THE HOMEOWNER'S

MINIMUM-MAINTENANCE

MANUAL

THE
HOMEOWNER'S
MINIMUM-
MAINTENANCE
MANUAL

by Stanley Schuler

PUBLISHED BY
M. Evans and Company, Inc., New York
AND DISTRIBUTED BY
J. B. Lippincott Company, Philadelphia and New York

Contents

THE HOMEOWNER'S

MINIMUM-MAINTENANCE

MANUAL

1

The Home-Maintenance
Headache and a
Few Basic Things You
Can Do to Make It
Less Painful

All of a sudden, the job of maintaining the home has taken on formidable new proportions.

In a way, this is rather strange. Man has been maintaining his home ever since he first took up living in a cave. It was just something he had to do to keep his abode habitable. And ever since then, maintenance has been just that—a routine requirement of life. Not a terribly demanding problem. Simply a dull chore.

But today, seemingly without warning, it has become a headache.

The reasons—when you start looking for them—are obvious:

* Better than half of the houses in the United States were built since World War II, and all too many of them were put up so hastily and cheaply that maintenance problems were bound to increase.

* Mechanical devices in the home not only have proliferated but also have grown steadily more complex.

* Despite a dramatic increase in the size of the so-called service industries, it is getting harder and harder to find men to do repair and maintenance work in the home; and if and when they do deign to put in an appearance, they often do their work poorly.

    * The cost of maintenance services is soaring. For example, from 1964 to 1969, the cost of replacing a sink rose 40.2 per cent; reshingling a roof, 40.3 per cent; repairing a furnace, 44.3 per cent; repainting a room, 50.4 per cent.

"I've gotten so discouraged with the way things are forever breaking down and needing repairs that no one wants to make," my dentist said to me recently, "that I don't even bother to try fixing equipment any more. I just throw it out and go down to a discount house and buy a replacement."

That, of course, is an extreme solution to the problem; and it is not one that many homeowners are likely to adopt. But I must say that the fourth time after I called in a serviceman to fix my brand-new refrigerator, I began to wonder whether it might not be a good idea to junk it before the warranty ran out.

A more practical approach to the home-maintenance problem is set forth on the following pages. It entails three steps: First, you should recognize why houses and their furnishings require maintenance. Then you should do everything possible to forestall the need for maintenance or, failing that, to minimize the amount of maintenance. Finally, you should adopt the maintenance methods which give best results with least work.

Why homes require maintenance

Home-maintenance is the process of constantly keeping all parts of your home, including the furnishings, in safe, sound and reasonably attractive condition. It maintains the value of your property. It permits you to live at a more or less constant level of comfort and convenience. It helps to protect you, your family and everyone setting foot in the house against unpleasant accidents. And it prevents secondary damage to your home (for example, when a corroded pipe breaks in an upstairs bathroom, you must not only fix the pipe, but you may also have to fix ceilings, walls and furniture wrecked by water gushing from the pipe).

Home maintenance becomes necessary because the materials, equipment and furnishings in a home do not last forever. They deteriorate for various reasons.

Some just wear out from usage. Automatic washing machines, for example, last an average of ten years, and there is little anyone can do to extend their life appreciably beyond that.

Some things wear out because of the abuse they are given by the occupants of the home. Screen doors and wallpaper are good examples.

Some things are worn out by the agents to which we unwittingly or deliberately expose them. Varnish on cabinet doors, for example, is damaged by the oils left on them by hands.

Some things are worn out by natural and unnatural phenomena—rain, heat, ice, or air polluted by millions of motor vehicles.

That there is no complete defense against the deterioration and ultimate breakdown of the home is evident. At least there is no affordable defense. But as I indicated earlier, there are many partial measures you can take which will help considerably. These are discussed in the three chapters immediately following.

Before we get to them, however, let's consider several assorted but important matters:

Budget for maintenance realistically

Home maintenance involves three kinds of work: (1) Preventive measures designed to avert or minimize material and equipment failures. (2) Simple measures, such as cleaning and lubricating, needed to keep things in good condition. (3) Repairs and renovations needed to set things right once trouble does arise.

It's perfectly obvious that the cost of doing these things varies with the age, size and construction of the house; the amount of mechanical equipment in it; the type of furnishings; the age, health and affluence of the homeowners; how much of the work the owners themselves do; and so on. But on the strength of research, which I and others have done, I have arrived at two average figures which the majority of homeowners should be safe in using:

If your house is less than five years old, budget your annual cost of maintenance at 6 per cent of the total cost of owning your home. (To figure the actual amount, add together the cost of mortgage payments, property tax, insurance, heat and other utilities and divide by 0.94. This gives you the total cost of home ownership. The amount in excess of the dividend of your division equals your maintenance budget.)

If your house is five years old or older, budget your annual cost of maintenance at 15 per cent of the total cost of owning your home. (To figure the amount, add together the costs named above and divide by 0.85.)

If you are lucky enough not to have a mortgage, budget your annual cost of maintenance at 15 per cent of total ownership costs (property tax, insurance, maintenance, heat and other utilities) if your house is less than five years old. For a house five years old or older, budget at 35 per cent.

For example, if in 1970 you owned an average house costing $26,000, your annual payments for mortgage, property tax, insurance, heat and other utilities totaled approximately $2520. So if your house was less than five years old, you should have budgeted $160 for maintenance. If it was more than five years old, you should have budgeted $445.

There are several additional points about budgeting for maintenance which should also be considered:

1. At the end of a year, when adding up how much it cost to maintain your home, consider the work you did on your furnishings and equipment as well as on the house itself. If you also want to add in the cost of maintaining your grounds, there is no reason why you should not do so. In this case, however, you should increase your maintenance budget about 3 percentage points.

2. Costs that should be charged against maintenance are for repairs, cleaning and other maintenance services, service

contracts, and cleaning and other maintenance supplies. Improvements should also be charged against maintenance to the extent that they were made to prevent future maintenance. For example, if you put aluminum siding on your house with the sole intention of cutting painting costs, I believe that the entire cost of the siding is a maintenance expense. (The Internal Revenue Service does not agree.) Or if you buy an awning for a window partly to make the room more comfortable and partly to keep the sun from fading the carpet, about half of the cost is chargeable to maintenance.

3. Many people are surprised to find that, while a new house requires less maintenance than an old house, it does nevertheless require it. The explanation is quite simple: All new houses develop flaws that call for repair and adjustment; and most of them contain old furnishings and appliances which also demand attention. Furthermore, the need for routine, housework-type maintenance is just as great in a new house as in an old. In fact, when my wife and I built a new house some years ago, we found we spent more for cleaning and floor waxing than ever before—probably because we were taking extra pains to keep the house looking new.

4. The budget figures recommended on the preceding page represent the average of the expenditures made over a period of years. Actually, once your house attains five years of age, you will find that you spend well under your budget one year and then go way over it the next. The best way to spare yourself the shock of those sky-high figures is to carry over to the next year any savings you have enjoyed in the preceding years.

Keep a fact book about your home

Suppose your new refrigerator needs service. Do you have the sales slip that proves it is still in warranty and that the factory must pay for repairs?

Or suppose the specially mixed paint you used on the living-room woodwork becomes marred in several spots. Do you have a wet sample in a can that the dealer can use to mix new paint to an exact match?

It pays to keep records about the materials, equipment and furnishings in your house. The following are especially useful:

Manufacturers' guarantees.

Sales slips on all items that are guaranteed.

Contracts with contractors, suppliers, etc.

Detailed blueprints and specifications for a house that was custom-built for you. If you buy a speculatively built house, ask the builder for a list of the manufacturers who produced the materials and equipment in the house.

Manufacturers' instruction and use-and-care booklets.

Paint samples in cans (it's much easier for a paint dealer to match wet paint than a dry chip).

Wallpaper samples showing the run numbers. (True, wallpaper firms generally do not keep patterns in stock or in production for very long but you can never be sure about this.)

Samples of all finish materials such as resilient flooring, ceramic tile, etc.

Names of all contractors, subcontractors, suppliers, etc. you dealt with when building.

Make an annual checkup of your home

It will help to forestall future trouble.

Of course, you don't need to make the checkup all at once. But at some time during the year you should inspect all parts of your home and correct problems that exist or may soon arise. Among the more important things to note and to do are the following (these and other points are covered at greater length in Chapter 5):

Replace damaged roofing materials. Carefully examine valley flashings for leaks.

Cut off weak tree limbs overhanging the roof.

Clean gutters and leaders. Rehang any that have become damaged.

Secure the TV antenna.

Secure loose siding. Fill cracks and open joints with calking compound.

Replace rotten wood wherever you find it.

Point up cracks in masonry.

Scrub efflorescence from masonry surfaces.

Stop leaks through foundation walls.

Look for termites and inject chlordane into the ground around
foundation walls every five to ten years.

Make sure that rain water drains rapidly away from foundation
walls and does not flood areaways.

Repair screens and storm sash.

Grease garage doors.

Tighten loose railings inside and outside.

Replace loose outside stair treads.

Fill holes and cracks in terraces, walks, driveways.

Clean out septic tank.

Close and drain outdoor faucets and pipelines.

Check all piping, especially at joints, for leaks.

Clean out traps below plumbing fixtures.

Have heating plant serviced.

Have chimney and furnace and water-heater flues cleaned.

Replace cracked windowpanes. Reputty.

Fix doors and windows that stick, rattle, don't close, etc.

Repair broken ventilating louvers through which squirrels and
other rodents may enter.

Fill holes, cracks and dents in interior walls.

Set popped nails in gypsum board.

Repaint walls, trim, etc.

Nail down loose floor boards.

Refinish floors.

Shore up sagging joists with lally columns.

Replace defective switches and outlets.

Replace cracked and stiffened extension cords.

Glue loose joints in furniture—especially chairs, which are particularly prone to break.

Hire help carefully

This has been said so often in magazines and books that I
am not going to stress the point here. But I can't ignore the
rule entirely because the sad truth is that millions of homeowners—despite repeated warnings—continue to hire repair-
men and servicemen without trying to find out anything
about them. As a result, they often get shoddy and sometimes
fraudulent work which has to be done over again and which
may also bring on other even worse maintenance problems.

In other words, when you hire some one to do maintenance work, make sure he is competent, responsible and
honest. Follow these eight simple rules:

1. Never employ a contractor who is represented by a high-pressure door-to-door salesman or who takes space in newspapers to advertise the application of "new, miracle" products.

2. Before hiring a man, find out what his previous customers think of him.

3. If for some reason you cannot learn anything about him, ask your Better Business Bureau for information.

4. On all big repair jobs get two or three bids.

5. Be sure you have a clear understanding of a contract before signing it.

6. Get any guarantee that is given in writing.

7. Don't make final payment until you are satisfied with the work.

8. If you have a legitimate complaint about anyone who does work for you, pass it on to the Better Business Bureau so they can warn others in the community.

2

Build Right to
Reduce Maintenance

The most important phase of all maintenance programs—whether they be for homes, factories, office buildings or what have you—comes under the heading of *preventive* maintenance.

As I said in Chapter 1, preventive maintenance is work designed to avert or minimize future trouble.

Industrial-maintenance men, for instance, make a practice of replacing all fluorescent tubes in their buildings at one time shortly *before* the tubes start to fail. To a thrifty homeowner, this may sound like an extravagant measure. But experience has taught the industrial-maintenance manager that it actually saves money in the form of labor costs because it is cheaper for a man to replace all fluorescent tubes at once than it is for him to run back and forth replacing each tube separately as it burns out.

In other words, this is a practice which involves work and expense but which *prevents* still greater work and expense.

Unfortunately, it is not a practice recommended to homeowners because we do not burn all lights in a house at the same time and for the same length of time. But there are many other preventive maintenance ideas which *do* apply to homeowners.

In this first of three chapters presenting these ideas, we start at bedrock—with the things you can do to avoid or minimize future maintenance by siting, designing and building your house properly in the first place.

At a glance, this chapter might appear to be of interest to you only if you are going to custom-build a new house. And I am free to admit that there are suggestions here which do apply only to the new home builder.

But there are also a number of suggestions which apply equally to people who are going to remodel their homes. And there are even some which might inspire you to undertake work on your present home purely and simply to reduce your maintenance load.

However you make use of this chapter, there are two basic points which must be noted at the outset:

1. You can't have easy maintenance without, to a certain extent, sacrificing something else—perhaps beauty, perhaps comfort, perhaps convenience.

2. Easy maintenance does not always come cheap. On the contrary, its original cost may be rather high. This explains why homes are rarely, if ever, as maintenance-free as offices, schools, factories, etc. No matter how badly home-owners want to reduce upkeep, they simply cannot bring themselves to make the sacrifices necessary to achieve perfection.

This does not mean, however, that you should not consider all the possibilities, regardless of how absurd some of them may seem. *You can save money in the long run* if you, your architect and your contractor plan, equip and furnish your home with its future maintenance very much in mind. (And you will be delighted to find that the occasional compromises you must make to achieve easy maintenance do not—or need not—detract seriously from your home in other ways.)

Choose your home location with care

The effect that environment has on home maintenance struck me hardest when my wife and I built a house in a hillside meadow some years ago. Before that, we had lived for twenty years in a big, old house which demanded about as much upkeep as a country home can; and our decision to build stemmed in part from this. But the positive steps we took in the new house to improve on the old were to considerable extent negated by our choice of location.

The wind that swept across the meadow from the northwest was constant and often fierce; and even though we were out in the country, surrounded by grass and beyond that woods, the house seemed to be inundated with dust and dirt. Whether this was actually the case or whether the dirt just appeared excessive because we didn't expect it in a new house and because it showed up more prominently, I am not now sure. But it is worth noting that since we moved again—to an old house which is not buffeted by wind—dirt and dust bother us little.

Wind, of course, is just one of the environmental factors that affect home maintenance. Rain, sleet, snow, hail, humidity, ground water, soot and chemicals in the air, heat, cold, sunlight, soil, vegetation, traffic are some of the others. By themselves they ordinarily cause trouble only if they can be described as unusual. (Traffic, for instance, rarely creates maintenance problems except in locations where it is heavy enough to stur up dust and pollute the air with the by-products of combustion.) But in combination, a little of this added to a little of that may be devastating. (It does not take very much rain and very many leaves to clog a gutter.)

Considered strictly from the maintenance standpoint, the most desirable location for a home is in the country about twenty-five miles upwind from any city or industrial area. The climate is moderate; the soil well drained and covered with vegetation; and all large trees are well removed from the house.

The most unfortunate locations include the open desert;

within a quarter mile of the ocean; an industrial area; a region with frequent hailstorms; a dense woodland (unless the trees around the house are cleared away); on poorly drained soil; on filled land or other unstable soil.

Adapt the house to any difficult conditions it must face

When hurricane Camille roared into the Mississippi coast in the late summer of 1969, I thought instantly of an older cousin whose home is within two hundred feet of the Gulf of Mexico; but I was not too worried for her, because although the house is now ramshackle, her father built it near the turn of the century just in anticipation of storms like Camille. It is so solid that I doubt whether anything short of dynamite could bring it down.

By contrast, earlier the same year, a friend who has a summer home in northern Vermont wrote that, although her new house had come through the winter unscathed, the heavy snows had crushed the roofs of some neighboring cottages.

Such things obviously should not happen. And there is no possible excuse why anyone should let them happen.

You do not have to be a genius to figure out what, if any, severe natural problems your home must cope with; and then to design the house to take them in stride.

If the annual snowfall is often very heavy, put extra bracing in the roof.

If flooding is common, raise the house off the ground on piers.

If the air is filled with soot, seal your windows and put in a central air conditioner.

If you build near the seashore, make flashing, gutters, leaders, window frames, screens, door hardware, etc. of materials or alloys that are not corroded by salt spray and air.

If the soil is unstable, have it tested to determine the type of footings you need to support the house permanently.

And so it goes.

Build on one floor

Daily tidying-up and weekly cleaning are easier just because you don't have to lug cleaning equipment up and down stairs. Such chores as gutter cleaning, window washing, screen hanging and exterior painting are much easier because you don't have to climb a tall ladder. And elimination of the stairway eliminates an architectural feature which takes exceptionally hard punishment and needs much maintenance as a result.

Keep outside dirt outside

Except for soot that drifts in through the windows, most of the dirt that accumulates in a house comes in through the front door, back and garage doors. The creatures that are most likely to bring it in are, in descending order, dogs, children, husbands and wives.

Housewives can talk themselves blue in the face trying to persuade the other members of the family that they really ought to wipe their feet before they come indoors. And even if they succeed at this, they are almost powerless to keep out the dirt that comes in on clothes and fur above the soles of the feet.

The only real defense against outside dirt, in short, is to plan the house so that dirt will not be tracked into it.

1. Lay out the rooms so that you need not walk through one part of the house to get to another. The easiest way to do this is to arrange the living area, sleeping areas and kitchen-dining area around a central hall. The front door opens into the hall; the back and garage doors open either into the hall or into the kitchen, which in turn opens into the hall.

2. Put a coat closet within a few feet of the front door. Put a second coat closet close to the back door, which children use most often.

3. Build a mudroom between the back door and the main part of the house. It is even better than a back-door coat

15

closet because it keeps dirt and wet clothes completely confined. Such a room is especially useful if you have a swimming pool but not a bathhouse, because you can rub more or less completely dry and knock the grass and dirt from your feet before going on to the bedroom area.

4. Build a vestibule outside your front entrance. It serves much the same purpose as a mudroom.

Build a watertight basement

As a potential cause of maintenance problems, a basement ranks below a roof; but while everyone recognizes the dangers inherent in a roof and takes pains to build a tight one, an awful lot of sloppy work goes into the construction of basements. In consequence, basements often leak and require attention; the furnace may be flooded; tools rust; and mildew attacks the rest of the house.

These problems are avoidable, however.

If you build on ground that has springs or a high water table, the basement walls should be made of poured, reinforced concrete. Provided these do not settle and develop cracks, they are completely waterproof. Concrete-block walls are much more likely to leak because the joints are not always well made. Unfortunately, this fact does not discourage the average builder from constructing block walls, even in very questionable situations. So it is up to you to see that they are waterproofed as much as possible before the soil is filled in behind them. The job is done by covering the outside of the walls from top to bottom with ½-inch concrete plaster applied in two equal coats. After the plaster dries, it is covered from the ground level down with one or two coats of bituminous compound.

To carry off water that settles in the ground next to basement walls, lay a continuous line of four-inch, perforated drainpipe alongside the footings. Cover the pipe with a thick layer of crushed rock, and slope the pipe toward a line of unperforated pipe which carries the water away from the house to a storm sewer, dry well, pond or stream.

The basement floor should be made of four-inch reinforced concrete poured over a vapor barrier of polyethylene film. The film is, in turn, laid over a six- to twelve-inch base of crushed rock.

Final step in the waterproofing job—and a very important one—is to slope the ground at grade level away from the basement walls. Hillside houses are protected on the uphill side by building diversion ditches across the hill to carry water around the side of the house. A flat space should also be provided between the hill and the house so that water can be collected in a storm drain and piped away.

If windows in the basement walls open into areaways, steps must be taken to keep the areaways from filling with water running across the ground. (Comparatively little falls in from the sky or roof, although a leaky gutter directly overhead might cause flooding.) One obvious step is to build up the top edges of the areaway about two inches above ground level. This alone should prevent trouble if your soil is reasonably porous; but if it is dense clay, install a drain from the areaway down to the footing drain. The top of the pipe should be several inches above the bottom of the areaway but below the window ledge, and should be covered with a wire strainer. Cover the areaway with coarse screen wire to keep out leaves and trash, if trees and shrubs are nearby.

Provide access to and headroom in all crawl spaces

This does not reduce maintenance to any appreciable extent (except by improving air circulation under the house). But it saves no end of trouble when it becomes necessary to crawl under the house to fix pipes, shore up joists, stop squeaks in floors or find a cat that decides to bring forth a litter in the most inaccessible spot she can think of.

All you need to do is provide at least eighteen inches of headroom—but preferably more—between the bottom of the crawl space and the joists above. And leave wide openings in foundation walls which separate one crawl-space area from another.

17

Control condensation

Condensation occurs in winter when the water vapor in the air inside your house strikes the chilled outer surfaces of the house. On windows, the film of water which forms is clearly visible but relatively harmless except for the eroding effect it has on paint and stain on the horizontal mullions and sills. But when condensation forms inside exterior walls and in unheated roof spaces and crawl spaces where you cannot see it, it may cause serious rotting of wood, corrosion of BX cables and blistering and peeling of exterior paint.

Control is essential. It includes the following measures:

1. Because crawl spaces are often a major source of the water vapor which permeates homes, you must make certain that the ground outside them slopes away from the house. Surface the bottom of each crawl space with concrete or a continuous sheet of heavy polyethylene film. Provide at least one screened, ventilated opening at the top of foundation walls enclosing the crawl space.

2. Insulate exterior walls, top-floor ceilings or attic spaces, and floors over unheated crawl spaces. This keeps the inner surfaces of these structures warm and thus prevents condensation from forming on them. It also conserves heat in winter and reduces the air-conditioning load in summer.

3. In cold climates, you should also double-glaze all windows and equip glass exterior doors with storm doors.

4. Provide a continuous vapor barrier on the inside of all exterior walls, top-floor ceilings, and floors over unheated crawl spaces. In a new house, vapor barriers are best made of sheets of polyethylene film stapled to the inner sides of studs and joists. Many insulating materials also contain effective built-in vapor barriers. In using any sheet-type barrier, make sure that all joints are lapped and securely fastened.

In an existing house, the most practical form of vapor barrier consists of two or three coats of alkyd or latex paint, varnish, shellac or floor seal. Vinyl wallcoverings and vinyl-coated wallpapers are also excellent. (Any of these may be used in a new house, too.)

5. If insulation and a vapor barrier are installed between the living areas and an unheated attic or roof space, there is little danger of water vapor entering the attic or roof space; consequently there is no need to make provision for water vapor to escape from these spaces. However, screened ventilators are required to allow hot air to escape in summer. The ventilators also serve as a safety valve just in case any moisture seeps upward past the vapor barrier.

6. Provide means for water vapor to escape from the laundry and bathrooms. (Kitchen ventilation—also very important—is discussed on page 40.) In the laundry, the principal source of moisture—and the only one you really must worry about—is the automatic dryer. The most efficient way to get rid of the moisture it generates is to extend a plastic or metal vent pipe from one of the exhaust openings in the back or sides of the dryer through an outside wall. The pipe should not exceed ten feet in length and should be as straight as possible. Easy-to-install vent kits are available from dryer retailers.

If for some reason it is not feasible to vent a dryer directly to the outdoors, an exhaust fan should be installed in an exterior wall of the laundry room.

Inside bathrooms must always be equipped with exhaust fans to carry off water vapor and odors. Outside bathrooms, however, are rarely ventilated by anything other than a window. But installation of a small exhaust fan is recommended in all exterior bathrooms which are heated by electricity or which are used by family members who delight in taking long, soaking, hot showers.

Stop termites

It is estimated that termite damage now costs Americans in the neighborhood of $350,000,000 a year. Although the damage is greatest in the southeast and California, homeowners in every state except Alaska are having trouble. What's even more surprising—new homes are under heavier attack than old.

The best way to control termites is to build a house so they can't get in. The following measures are required in all areas south of the 43d parallel:

1. If the house has a basement or crawl space, build foundation walls of poured concrete or cap concrete-block walls with a continuous four-inch slab of poured concrete. The sills atop the walls should be at least eight inches above grade. Wood siding should be at least six inches above grade. Joists should be at least eighteen inches above the bottom of any crawl spaces.

2. If the house is built on a slab, the slab should be either of the monolithic or suspended type, and the top should be at least eight inches above grade. The siding should not come within six inches of the ground. (Slabs constructed so that there is a vertical joint between the slab edges and the footings are rarely termite-proof.)

3. No matter what kind of slab is constructed, treat the soil under and around it with chlordane. Houses built over crawl spaces will also benefit by this soil treatment, though it is unnecessary if the foundation walls are built in the way described above.

4. Remove all construction lumber, roots, paper and other cellulose debris from the soil under and around the house. It attracts termites.

5. Raise all wood posts, steps, storage closets, etc. at least six inches off the ground on masonry or metal bases. Do not allow masonry steps, terraces or the like to butt directly against the framing or wood siding of the house. Do not connect subsidiary wood structures, such as fences and arbors, to the house unless they, too, are raised off the ground on masonry bases.

Use of framing lumber that is pressure-treated with wood preservative is an additional safeguard against termites. In fact, if such lumber is used throughout a slab house from the sills up to the ceiling joists of the first floor, or if it is used throughout a house built over a basement or crawl space up to the finish floor, no additional control measures are required. However, treated lumber is so much more expensive you are not likely to use it except in isolated places where other control measures are impossible to carry out.

In existing houses, termite protection starts with removing all cellulose material from the soil around and under the house; making sure that water drains away from the house and does not get into crawl spaces; plugging all cracks and holes in foundation walls and slabs; and breaking the contact between the ground and any wood parts of the house or connected substructures.

Once you have taken these steps, you should treat the soil around and under the house with chlordane or an equivalent chemical. Since this is arduous work—and extremely difficult in the case of houses built on slabs—you will be smart to employ a recommended termite-control firm to do it for you.

Almost all firms guarantee soil treatments for five years. Extensive testing by government experts and others, however, indicates that recommended chemicals currently in use actually are effective for ten years or longer.

Install gutters—or should you?

This is a question that can be debated forever. The great value of gutters is that they carry the rain water falling on the roof away from the house (at least they do this if you connect the leaders into the footing drains or install sloping drainage basins at their base). But their great drawback is that they become clogged with leaves and twigs and need periodic cleaning out; and they occasionally need to be straightened, rehung and repaired.

The principal reason for not installing gutters is to improve the appearance of the roof line. They are not very attractive under any circumstances; and on contemporary and modern houses, they are an eyesore. But if you don't have them, you are in for a variety of headaches which may well prove more aggravating than simple gutter maintenance but which recur less frequently: The rain dripping and cascading from the roof edges damages planting material underneath and even beats a bare strip in the soil. On windy days, dripping water is blown back against the wall and windows, streaking them and working in through cracks around the sash. Finally the water sinks into the ground around the house and leaks through foundation walls.

Happily for the adherents of gutterless homes, the latter problems can be solved (1) if you build a house with such wide eaves—at least three feet—that the dripping water is rarely blown back against the walls and falls to the ground well away from the foundations and (2) if you install a paved or gravel strip under the eaves and leading away to some sort of drainage basin.

Gutter-maintenance problems are not solved quite so easily. The wire strainers which are stuck into the openings of leaders keep the leaders from clogging but not the gutters, Six-inch-wide strips of wire or plastic mesh which are laid over gutters do a good job of keeping out leaves but are not so effective against twigs, seeds, roofing granules, etc. Yet there can be no doubt that gutters are a necessity on a house with narrow eaves—and especially if the house is two stories high, because the extra height increases the likelihood that water will be blown against the walls. Gutters are also necessary if the ground around the house defies drainage.

On the other hand, you should think twice about putting gutters on *any* house that is overhung with large trees.

Keep sun and rain off windows

The sun fades and bleaches materials and finishes inside the house, causing a costly replacement or refinishing problem. Rain water-spots and streaks the glass, necessitating frequent washing in urban areas and occasional washing elsewhere.

Fortunately, in most parts of the country, sun fading is encountered mainly at south windows and to a lesser extent at east and west windows. Only in southern latitudes do you get any fading at north windows.

Rain, on the other hand, strikes all windows everywhere.

Since the best protection against rain is a wide eave, wide eyebrow or awning, and since these devices also give good protection against sun, they should be used on all sides of your house. But in dry climates where the sun is much more troublesome than rain, you may prefer to use tinted glass. This, of course, distorts the color of the landscape, and it water-spots like ordinary glass, but it substantially reduces the ultraviolet radiation which causes fading.

A more radical way of reducing fading and window-spotting is to install skylights with diffusing glass or plastic rather than windows. Skylights require little maintenance, admit more light and give better light distribution than windows. But of course they have a number of drawbacks.

Use the right fasteners (nails, screws, etc.)

They hold better and resist corrosion.

Only galvanized steel nails and galvanized or brass screws and bolts should be used on the exterior of the house because they will not rust and stain siding and trim. (This is true whether they are countersunk or not.) Of course, steel nails ought not to rust either if they are countersunk and covered with putty. But, unfortunately, the puttying is usually done not by the carpenters who drive and countersink the nails, but by painters; and unless the painters follow hard on the heels of the carpenters, the nailheads soon become rusty. Once that happens, no amount of putty will stop the rust from bleeding through and pockmarking your house with unsightly brown stains.

Inside the house, corrosion of fasteners is rare so you can use those made of any strong, durable material. But in several situations it is very important to use fasteners of the right kind.

For example, gypsum board should always be installed with ring-grooved nails. Any other kind—including the cement-coated nails which sheetrockers usually use—is likely to "pop"; pull loose from the studs and joists and blister or even break through the wall or ceiling surfaces.

23

Towel rods, soap dishes and similar fittings which may be subjected to weight or pressure should be hung on gypsum board, hardboard and very thin plywood walls with split-wing toggle bolts or hollow-wall screw anchors. Ordinary screws can be used only in thick wood or plaster walls, or if the towel-rod holders are installed directly over studs.

Objects hung on masonry walls inside or outside the house are generally best secured with screws driven into lead anchors.

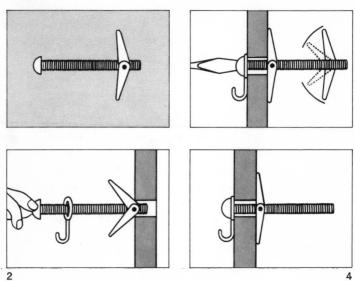

2   4

Installing a toggle bolt.

Install single-pane windows

Although you are more conscious of spots and streaks on them than on multipane windows, they can be washed much more quickly. One manufacturer, in fact, claims that whereas it takes 10 minutes and 29 seconds to wash both sides of a twelve-pane window, it takes only 5 minutes and 13 seconds to wash a single-pane window of the same dimensions. I question the figures but not the conclusion.

The snap-in mullions turn large, single-paned windows into multi-paned windows. They can be removed for easy cleaning. (Anderson Corp.)

If the style of your house requires multipane windows, put in single-pane windows anyway and make them look like multipane windows with removable mullions. Be sure, however, that the mullions are made of vinyl molded in one piece. These are not completely resistant to breakage, but they are considerably sturdier than snap-in mullions made of wood or of vinyl with pinned joints.

Prepare a sound base for all flooring materials

The difficulties of maintaining floors depend mainly on the materials with which the floors are surfaced (pages 67–73). But some maintenance work may also result if the base for the flooring materials is carelessly constructed. The following points should be borne in mind:

Resilient flooring materials should never be laid on concrete until a moisture test of the concrete has been made. If moisture is found to be present, you must delay completing the floor.

To prepare an old concrete slab for resilient flooring, remove all grease and paint; fill cracks; grind down raised and rough spots; level low spots with mastic underlayment; take up all dust and dirt in a vacuum; then apply size to the entire slab.

Do not lay resilient flooring directly over old. Either scrape up the old material or cover it with quarter-inch hardboard, plywood or chipboard underlayment.

Do not lay resilient flooring on a board floor unless the boards are less than three inches wide and laid atop a subfloor. If the board floor is only a single thickness or made of boards more than three inches wide, it should be covered with a rigid underlayment at least a quarter inch thick.

The base for seamless flooring must be prepared in about the same way. However, most manufacturers recommend against laying a floor of this kind on any type of board floor. And all joints on the subfloor must be filled.

To lay a strip-wood floor over a concrete slab poured on

Prepare a sound base for flooring materials
When a wood subfloor is only a single layer, or double-layer floor
boards are in bad condition, the floor should be covered with a
rigid underlayment before resilient or seamless flooring is installed. (Armstrong Cork Co.)

or below grade, lay one-inch wood sleepers which are pressure-treated with preservative in mastic on the slab. Cover with a vapor barrier of heavy polyethylene film. Lay a second set of sleepers over the first. Then apply the flooring strips at right angles to the sleepers.

Install cove-base strips in the kitchen

They are also a good idea in bathrooms, laundries and other rooms—wherever resilient or seamless floors are used.

Made of rubber or vinyl, the concave strips take the place of baseboards. By eliminating the sharp right-angle bend usually found between floor and wall, the strips greatly simplify floor-mopping. They also protect the base of walls and toeboards under kitchen cabinets from scuffing.

If you do not like the appearance of cove-base strips, you can still accomplish what they are designed to do by having sheet vinyl or other sheet-style flooring materials curved up the walls for four inches or more. This is called a "flash-type cove base."

Seamless flooring is curved up walls in the same way.

If you use resilient floor tiles instead of sheet materials, you can use cove-base strips or you can paste half tiles to the base of walls and cabinet toeboards. These give good protection against scuffing but do not, of course, eliminate the hard-to-clean right-angle bend.

Prepare carefully for paint and wallpaper

Painting and wallpapering are essentially simple jobs; and homeowners quite properly take it pretty much for granted that the professionals they employ will do the work well. But the truth is that professionals are as capable of slipshod work as the rankest amateur. So when it comes to decorating your house inside or out, it behooves you to give as much thought to the preparations that are made as to the materials that are used. Failing to do this, you may discover to your sorrow that the work must be redone very soon.

Cove base strip of vinyl protects the wall against scarring and is rounded at the floor line to eliminate a dirt catching corner. (Armstrong Cork Co.)

Here is an assortment of facts you should know:

As a rule, exterior paint should be allowed to weather three or four years before a house is repainted; otherwise the new paint is likely not to adhere properly (see page 160).

The finish coat on the exterior of the house must be applied within two weeks of the prime coat. If more time is allowed, the finish coat may flake off. (This rule is very commonly ignored by professional painters.)

Exterior paint is best applied in dry weather when the temperature is between 50 and 80 degrees. There should be little wind (especially if the ground is bare and dusty) and few insects. If insects are present, do not burn lights— outdoors or in—which will attract them at night to newly painted surfaces.

If you want to preserve the original natural appearance of wood on the exterior of the house, apply a clear wood preservative to redwood, a clear penetrating sealer to other kinds of wood. Unfortunately, sealers are short-lived and need to be reapplied every few years.

Before a new finish is applied, the old finish must be removed if it is blistered, flaking, chalking or badly cracked; if it is very thick; if it is scarred so deeply that the edges of the scar cannot be obliterated; or if it is whitewash or calcimine.

If nailheads are countersunk and covered with putty (see page 23), the putty should be applied after the wood is primed.

All knots should be primed before any other finish is applied with WP-578 knot sealer. This will keep the resin from bleeding through the final coat of paint.

Interior wood that has been coated with creosote stain should be primed with shellac to prevent bleeding. Creosote stain on exterior wood generally does not need to be primed if it has weathered for a year or more.

To keep the grain in fir plywood from spoiling the appearance of the paint, treat the plywood with a resin sealer before paint is applied.

Gypsum board must be given a priming coat before it is

wallpapered; otherwise, when the wallpaper is removed some day in the future, the paper surface of the gypsum board will come off, too.

Old wallpaper should be removed completely before new is applied.

Newly plastered walls should be tested for free lime (hot spots) before they are wallpapered. If hot spots show up, they should be treated with zinc sulfate solution.

If paint is to be applied over a surface that has ever been mildewed, a mildew retardant should be added to it. Visible mildew must, of course, be washed off the surface.

Use simple woodwork

Elaborately milled moldings, paneled doors, turned balusters, ornate mantels, etc. are dust-catchers to start with and hard to clean to boot. Furthermore, they are difficult to paint; and if it becomes necessary to remove the old finish before applying new, you are in for a struggle of mammoth proportions.

Simple, smooth-surfaced woodwork is easier all around. And it usually costs less.

Build wear-free stairs

Actually, this is impossible. All stairs take a beating. But you can reduce the wear they receive to some extent by the way you lay them out. Here's how:

1. Make them wider than usual (usual is 32 to 36 inches) and put railings on both sides. People who generally hold on to a railing when going up or down stairs walk fairly close to the railing. Those who don't use a railing usually walk in the middle of the stairs. This means that on a narrow stairway with one railing, the wear on the treads is concentrated from more or less the middle of the treads to the railing side. So by making stairs wider and installing two railings, you spread the wear on the treads and thus reduce maintenance of them.

2. Make stairways straight. When they turn corners or are curved, you cannot carry furniture and other large articles up and down without banging against the walls and balusters.

3. Provide as much headroom as possible. This also facilitates carrying furniture up and down stairs. According to the FHA, the minimum headroom on a main stairway should be 6 feet 8 inches. But on the average narrow stair this is probably not adequate for movement of very large articles such as king-size mattresses.

4. Eliminate risers. They usually show wear faster than treads because you hit them with the toes of your shoes as you go up and scuff them with your heels as you come down. By eliminating them, you substantially reduce the surface that has to be maintained. You also simplify vacuuming or sweeping of the stairs because there are no corners for dirt to hide in.

5. Eliminate balusters in the railing. They are tedious to paint. They are tedious to dust if they are turned. And they make tread and floor cleaning tedious beyond words. A railing that is supported only at the two ends is just about as strong and much, much easier on the homemaker.

Build in furniture

Built-ins save a certain amount of work because dust cannot collect under and behind them as it does with freestanding pieces. (However, one built-in that adds to housework is a built-in bed: it is fiendish to make.)

Put all items on shelves behind doors

You do this without a second thought in kitchens, closets and bathrooms. If you also did it for books, china and silver displayed in the dining room, and miscellaneous collections displayed elsewhere in the house, you would keep dust from collecting on them so rapidly.

Close in the space above kitchen wall cabinets

Object: to keep greasy dust from settling on them. The easiest way to do this is simply to nail hardboard or plywood to the top front edge of the cabinets and to a furring strip attached to the ceiling directly above. But the space may also be closed in behind sliding doors so that it can be used for dead storage of little-used utensils, appliances, etc.

Veto ornamental features requiring high maintenance

Here are some of the worst:

Shutters—especially louvered shutters.
Louvered doors. Like shutters, they are hard to clean and hard to paint. To be sure, new doors made of nylon are an improvement because they do not need refinishing; but they still catch dust.
Chair rails, which are also dust-catchers.
Wall paneling with inset panels.
And light coves, which are next to impossible to keep clean.

Build easier-to-clean bathrooms

The most maintenance-free bathroom you can buy is a "one-piece" unit molded out of fiberglass (see page 86). It is not pretty, however. Neither is it as luxurious as you might like. Consequently, I wouldn't blame you for preferring a conventional bathroom. But just because it is conventional does not mean it must be so difficult and disagreeable to keep in order as bathrooms usually are. You can improve matters in several ways:

1. Make the bathroom big enough so that you can clean under and behind the toilet and lavatory without tying yourself in knots.

2. Place the toilet in the middle of a wall, not in a corner where floor cleaning is difficult. For the same reason, don't put the toilet in a small alcove or compartment.

3. Install a wall-hung toilet. You can mop the floor under it with one quick swish.

33

4. Install a wall-hung lavatory, which is also easier to mop under. The alternative is to install the lavatory in a vanity cabinet which is built tight to the floor.

5. Install the soap dish and toothbrush holder directly over the lavatory so you don't drip water on the floor when you reach to them.

Guard your plumbing system against "difficult" water

Hard water builds up a scale deposit in pipes, water heaters and boilers, and thus reduces the flow of water and the efficiency of heating units. Iron-bearing water (as well as manganese-bearing water, which is less common) stains plumbing fixtures and may form a scale which constricts valves, etc. Corrosive water eats out pipe and tank metals and causes leaks. It is an especially serious troublemaker when heated.

Use of copper tube rather than galvanized pipe prevents or at least minimizes some of these problems. But your best defense, if tests prove your water is unusually hard or corrosive or carries a heavy concentration of iron, is to condition the water before it enters the main part of your plumbing system.

A zeolite water softener of the proper size is generally installed to remove hardness from water. Iron-bearing and corrosive waters are usually passed through neutralizing filters. To determine exactly what equipment you need, consult a plumbing contractor; and if he cannot help you, call in a water-conditioning dealer.

Regardless of how you condition your water, two other things that must be done to prevent corrosion of pipes are the following: (1) Never join together pipes or fittings of dissimilar metal (for example, steel and copper). Install a special insulating joint between the inlet and outlet pipes and the water heater if they are not of the same metal. (2) Do not install pipes of dissimilar metal in the same trench in the ground or close to each other; and don't lay steel pipe in cinders.

Install non-freezing outdoor faucets

You won't have to turn them off in the winter and on again in the spring.

Don't skimp on your septic system

Naturally if you live in a community with strong, rigorously enforced building and sanitary codes, you will not be allowed to skimp. In communities without such codes, however, many home builders knowingly or unknowingly put in inadequate septic systems. That inevitably leads to unnecessary maintenance and frequently creates health hazards.

Construction of a septic system is a fairly complicated business; and if any part is improperly built, maintenance work will result. But since this chapter is not meant to give specific building instructions, I shall not go into the detailed story of how to build septic systems. There are, however, three points you should understand:

1. The size of the tank you put in should be based on the number of bedrooms in the house. FHA standards require a tank of no less than 750 gallons. This is adequate for a one- or a two-bedroom house. For a three-bedroom house, you need a 900-gallon tank; four bedrooms, 1000 gallons; and for each additional bedroom add 250 gallons. FHA says these sizes are adequate for a house with or without a garbage disposer; but many communities require bigger tanks if you have a disposer.

2. The disposal field into which the effluent from the tank runs should not be located near trees, because the roots may invade and clog the pipelines. You should also avoid a location over which you might run a truck or heavy tractor that could break the pipelines.

3. The size of the disposal field (that is, the number of feet of pipe it contains) and the size and construction of the trenches in which the pipes are laid must be determined by a percolation test of the soil. The field size also depends on the

35

number of bedrooms in the house. Rules for making percolation tests and establishing the size of disposal fields are covered in FHA's *Minimum Property Standards.*

Air-condition the house

Then you will never have to open your windows. This will not only cut down on the amount of dirt that enters the house from outside, but it will also save you the trouble of keeping the windows in good operating order.

(Incidentally, if windows are never opened, the ideal kind to install are plate-glass units extending from the floor to the ceiling in uninterrupted sheets. These are easy to wash. In addition, they have no sill-like ledges, horizontal mullions or framing members that forever need dusting.)

Install an air cleaner

If operated continuously (for only a few cents a day), it will suck dust, smoke and grease particles out of the air before they have a chance to settle and collect on the many surfaces within the house.

Several types of air cleaner are available. All of those used for cleaning the air throughout an entire house must be tied into a ducted heating or air-conditioning system. Small, usually portable cleaners are big enough to clean the air only in one room and are used mainly by people with allergies.

The simplest of the central air cleaners is the filter with which warm-air furnaces are equipped. But it is also the least efficient since it traps only a small percentage of the dirt particles passing through it.

The next best air cleaner is known as a "charged-media" type. Consisting of a large mechanical filter which is charged with electricity, it removes between 40 and 70 per cent of the dirt particles passing through it. When the filter becomes dirty, it must be replaced.

By far the best air cleaner is a two-stage electronic device which may remove as much as 90 per cent of the dirt particles

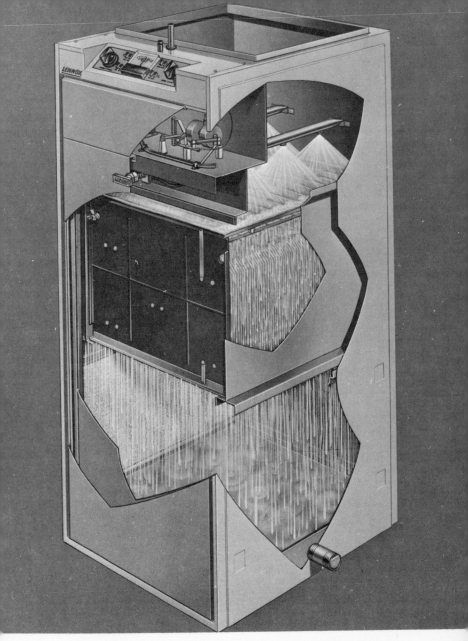

In this electronic air cleaner, air enters at the top, and as it moves through the ionizing screen (flat plate one-third down from top) the dirt, dust and pollen particles it contains receive a positive electrical charge. The particles then pass into the closely spaced, vertical collecting plates (center) to which they adhere. The clean air goes out through the bottom section and is recirculated through the house. The collector cells are washed every two weeks by sprays of water, as shown, and the water is drained off at the bottom. (Lennox Industries)

going through it. The cleaner traps the largest particles in a mechanical filter; the remainder on negatively charged plates in a collection chamber. Some models must be cleaned by hand about every three months. Others have automatic washing devices that free you of all work.

In buying an air cleaner, you should remember that it captures only the dirt particles passing through it. In other words, if the dealer says it has an efficiency rating of 85 per cent, that means it removes 85 per cent of the dirt particles that are in the air circulated through the cleaner. The rating figure used should be based on the U. S. Bureau of Standard's "Dust Spot" test.

Ratings which state the weight of the dirt collected by an air cleaner do not give an accurate picture of the cleaner's efficiency.

Maintain a proper indoor humidity

We all know that when air in a house is too dry, we feel uncomfortable; and when it is too damp, the house smells musty. But what many people fail to realize is that humidity also has a direct bearing on home upkeep.

If the air is dry, dirt particles break up into smaller particles which float through the air. Rugs and other fabrics may be filled with static electricity which attracts dirt like a magnet. The wood in the house and in the furnishings shrinks, develops cracks which do not always close up again, and sometimes disintegrates.

If the house air is too humid, on the other hand, the dirt particles that settle on fabrics soak in so completely that you can get them out only with a solvent. Mildew forms on painted surfaces, leather, books, etc. and stains them badly. Toilet tanks, water tanks and pipes sweat and drip.

How do you prevent these problems?

First of all, you should note that not every homeowner is bothered by too much or too little humidity. But if you put in a warm-air heating system, you can be pretty sure the house air will be too dry in winter. And if you live in a humid climate—and especially if you build in a low, damp spot or in a woodland—you can expect the house air will seem too damp in summer.

To humidify your house if you have a ducted heating system, you should attach a power humidifier to the furnace. This contains some sort of absorbent wheel or belt that picks up water from a pan and then gives off moisture to the air flowing past it. The best models are completely automatic in operation; and some even draw off and replace the water in the pan so that a lime deposit cannot build up. The absorbent pads must, however, be cleaned occasionally; and eventually they need to be replaced.

The other kind of humidifier commonly used in warm-air furnaces is an evaporative-plate type. These are less expensive than power humidifiers, but they are also much less desirable because they are rarely large enough to humidify a house properly. The plates must also be cleaned frequently.

If you do not have a ducted heating system, the best humidifier is a small atomizing unit which can be tucked into the top of a closet. It draws water from the plumbing system via a small copper tube; the atomized moisture issues as a barely visible fog through a vent in the closet. In hard-water areas, the water should first be passed through a demineralizer before entering the humidifier. This unit can also be installed so that it exhausts into the ductwork of a warm-air heating system.

All three of these built-in humidifiers should be controlled by an automatic humidistat.

A fourth type of humidifier is a portable unit (usually in a televisionlike console). These hold from about two to fifteen gallons of water, which are soaked up in a pad and then evaporated. The storage tanks are refilled by hand.

Dehumidification of house air is best done automatically by a central or room air conditioner. Lacking an air conditioner, you can buy a portable dehumidifier which plugs into any electric outlet. Depending on the size of the unit, it will remove up to eight gallons of water from the air per day. The water drains into a drip pan which must be emptied by hand, or into a hose that connects into the house drain.

Install a kitchen ventilating fan

You need it to capture grease vapors that otherwise collect on every kitchen surface and water vapor that condenses on windows and perhaps in walls. You also need it to get rid of cooking odors and smoke, but that's beside the point here.

Two kinds of ventilating fan are available: one is ducted to the outdoors; the other is not. Both types are enclosed in hoods which are suspended over the range. There are also simple ducted fans which are installed in walls or ceilings.

Of the two types, the ducted fan is much the better because it removes both grease and water vapor from the air (as well as odors and smoke) whereas the non-ducted fan removes grease only (plus odors and smoke). The choice between a ducted fan with hood and one without hood is also just as one-sided. The former pulls in more of the grease and water vapors given off during cooking operations because it hangs directly over the burners. And the grease it collects is much more easily cleaned out of the fan because it is trapped in an aluminum-mesh filter before it can get into the fan and duct-work.

If for some reason you cannot use a hood fan, the next choice is an ordinary fan installed in an exterior wall just above the range backsplash. I emphasize exterior wall because a fan in an interior wall must exhaust into a long and sometimes meandering duct, which is very difficult to clean when full of grease. In other words, if your kitchen plan calls for a range on an inside wall, you should either redraw the plan with the range on an exterior wall and install a wall fan above it, or you should use a hood fan.

Another alternative would be to install a non-ducted hood fan above the range and a ducted wall fan in an exterior wall. Naturally, this is extravagant, but it is probably the best of all kitchen-ventilating arrangements if your sink and dishwasher are not close to your range, because the wall fan can be placed to collect water vapor from all three appliances.

40

Luminous ceiling made by installing a bank of fluorescent tubes as above. A diffusing panel bathes a room in even, glareless light. Note that it even eliminates shadows under base cabinet toespace. (General Electric Co.)

Install good lighting

Good lighting reduces maintenance work because it permits you to see what needs to be done as well as what you are doing. It provides a level of illumination that allows you to see without straining. It brightens all corners of every room. It is relatively shadow-free and glareless.

Good lighting is most easily achieved by building light fixtures permanently into the house. (Portable lamps supplement built-in lights, but alone they almost never give adequate over-all light.) And the best place to install these fixtures is, first, at the ceiling level and, second, high up on large walls.

Of the many kinds of fixtures used, the luminous ceiling panel is outstanding because it covers a large ceiling area (sometimes the entire ceiling) and uses fluorescent lights. True, it is expensive, so you will not want to use it in every room. But it is especially desirable in rooms which get hard usage and which need frequent cleaning: kitchens, family rooms, bathrooms and central halls.

Because of the prejudice against using ceiling fixtures in living rooms and, to lesser extent, in dining rooms, these rooms are often lighted by fluorescent valances, wall brackets and cornices. Such fixtures are really nothing more than fluorescent tubes mounted horizontally high on a wall, and concealed behind a board about six inches wide. Valances and wall brackets are particularly desirable because they are installed about a foot below the ceiling and direct light both up on the ceiling and down on the wall or draperies below. Cornice lights mounted at the ceiling direct light downward only.

In bedrooms the simplest way to achieve a high level of general illumination is to install a ceiling fixture in the middle of the room. Fixtures suspended below the ceiling so that they throw light up, down and to the sides spread light better than recessed or surface-mounted fixtures which direct all light straight down. For this reason, when using the former, you need to provide only about one watt per square foot of room area, whereas with the latter you need about three watts per square foot. Furthermore, when using the former, you need only one fixture for each average-size bedroom whereas you should use two or three of the latter fixtures.

Install a central vacuum cleaner

This is a built-in system similar to central air conditioning. A large stationary unit including the motor and dirt receptacle is installed in the basement, utility room or garage. A network of tubes in the walls, floors and ceilings connect this unit to three or four vacuum inlets located at strategic points throughout the house. Cleaning tools consist of a long, flexible hose and various cleaning nozzles. When operating, the cleaner sucks the dirt from the house through the hose and ducts to the central tank.

A built-in vacuum-cleaning system does not relieve you of the necessity of moving the hose and cleaning nozzles from room to room, like an ordinary vacuum. But you must plug in the hose only three or four times; there is no need to plug and unplug an electric cord in every room you enter. The dirt receptacle needs to be emptied only a few times a year. Some systems, in fact, automatically carry the dirt off down a plumbing drain. Dust cannot re-enter the house whereas with an ordinary vacuum cleaner, a small amount of dust passes right through the machine back into the room in which it is being used.

3

Select Low-upkeep Materials, Equipment and Furnishings

Several years ago I became involved in a propaganda battle between the carpet and resilient-flooring industries. The fight —precipitated by the development of new kinds of carpet which for the first time were durable and economical enough for use in public and commercial buildings—centered mainly on the question of which general type of material was easier to maintain.

My job was to find out what education officials thought; and to that end I interviewed school-maintenance supervisors from one end of the country to the other. Not surprisingly I came up with a complete divergence of opinion. Some men favored carpet; some, resilient flooring; a few, terrazzo. Some opinions were based on prejudice and hunch; others, on actual experience. But even the latter were of dubious value because no two school systems kept maintenance records in the same way, had identical schools, followed the same maintenance procedures, etc.

Right here you get some idea of how difficult it often is to make a realistic evaluation of the amount of maintenance required by the different materials, equipment and furnishings you can choose between when you build, remodel or equip your house. A variety of points must be considered:

The purpose served by the item in question.

The conditions to which it will be subjected.

Its durability.

The frequency and extent to which it will need servicing and refinishing.

Its resistance to soiling.

Its cleanability.

The frequency with which it will need cleaning.

Its capability for creating secondary maintenance problems.

When you match this list against the many items in the home, it is obvious that the questions you ask about one are not necessarily the same as those you ask about something else. For example, if you're buying calking compound for use outside the house, your only real concern should be its durability when exposed to the conditions that prevail on your property. Its resistance to soiling and its cleanability are of no importance. On the other hand, when you buy furniture for a family room, every point on the list should be considered.

These differences in the criteria for judging materials, equipment and furnishings create one problem in evaluating their need for upkeep.

A second problem—for which there is no real solution—stems from the fact that many materials which are easy to clean demand more maintenance than those which are hard to clean. How come? Simply because they show dirt.

This is one of the arguments made for using carpet rather than, say, vinyl on kitchen floors. Carpet is harder to clean—or I should say: get really clean—than vinyl. But because it is soft and textured, you can't see dirt on it so clearly as on vinyl and therefore you may not feel pushed to clean it so often.

The patterns and colors of materials may also make a difference in your feelings about cleaning them. For instance, there is little doubt that a patterned material shows dirt less than a solid. So if you impose a pattern on a strongly textured material, such as kitchen carpet, you should be able to reduce kitchen floor upkeep still further. On the other hand, if your choice lay between a non-patterned carpet and a vinyl with a strong, indefinite pattern, the vinyl might show less dirt than the carpet.

You run up against a comparable sort of which-is-better question on the color front. Generally, very light-colored and very dark-colored materials show dirt more than medium tones. But in a beach house, you would be less aware of sand on a white floor than on a medium-blue floor; and if you lived on the edge of a peat bog, you'd be less aware of peaty dirt on a black floor than on a red one.

A third problem that complicates efforts to decide which materials, equipment and furnishings to use in your house was mentioned at the start of the previous chapter. I repeat it here because it is too basic to be ignored: Unless easy home maintenance is the be-all-and-end-all in your life, you cannot select things for your home without also giving thought to their initial cost, appearance, convenience, comfort, etc. In the end, these factors may outweigh or at least compromise your determination to have a completely maintenance-free home.

But that's enough about the problems of selecting easy-upkeep materials, etc. Let's get down to the brass tacks of what is good and what isn't so good. Here are two general guidelines:

Don't be influenced by the price of the thing you are considering

I think most people feel that high price stands for top quality, and that top quality just naturally stands for durability and easy maintenance. But while the first part of this belief is usually correct, the second part is not. Quality often stands for things which have nothing whatever to do with easy maintenance. Furthermore, quality is often to be found in materials and equipment which are relatively low in price.

For example, a low-cost automatic washer has as much quality as a high-cost washer built by the same manufacturer.

It just is a simpler machine without as many features. And because it is simpler, there are fewer things that can go wrong with it. Ergo: It is easier to maintain.

Or consider laminated plastics and ceramic tiles—both quality products. But a kitchen countertop made of ceramic tile costs more than one of laminated plastic and is more difficult to maintain.

I can give you other examples along the same line. In fact, if you analyze the entries on the pages following, you will find a total of twenty-four cases where a relatively low-cost product requires less maintenance than higher-cost products.

On the other hand, you will also find thirty-seven cases where a high-cost product requires less maintenance than lower-cost products. (In addition, you will find fifteen which are toss-ups.)

In short, as I said in the beginning, product cost is not a reliable indicator of product maintainability.

But pay attention to the way in which manufacturers guarantee their products

Of course, most home products are guaranteed only for durability. They are not ordinarily guaranteed, say, to shrug off dirt, or to be easy to clean, or to be incapable of causing secondary maintenance problems. So obviously, when you are trying to pick products which need little upkeep, you must not overstress the guarantee on them. On the other hand, since durability has such definite bearing on product maintenance, the guarantee must be considered carefully.

Note these points in particular:

The period for which the product is guaranteed. A water-heater tank guaranteed for ten years is almost certainly better than one which is guaranteed for only five years.

Any limitations on the guarantee. For example, some water-heater tanks are guaranteed for ten years but the guarantee is unconditional for only five years; in each succeeding year thereafter you get proportionally less credit. Such a guarantee is better than a simple five-year guarantee; but upon close examination, it does not look so good as it did originally.

AVERAGE LIFE EXPECTANCY OF VARIOUS COMPONENTS OF THE HOME

Asphalt shingle roof	20	years
Wood shingle roof	25–30	"
Built-up roof	20	"
Warm-air furnace	15	"
Hot-water boiler (cast iron)	30	"
Central air conditioner	12	"
Water heater (tank-type—best grade)	15	"
Water pump	20	"
Exterior paint	4– 6	"
Interior paint	6– 8	"
Vinyl floor	30	"
Vinyl-asbestos floor	30	"
Asphalt-tile floor	25	"
Carpet	12	"
Refrigerator	15	"
Range	20	"
Dishwasher	10	"
Automatic washer	10	"
Dryer	13	"
Television set	5	"
Upholstery on chair or sofa	6	"

The conditions of the guarantee. For example, a water heater might be guaranteed for ten years; but in order to collect, the buyer must return his defective heater to the maker. This is patently ridiculous. The manufacturer knows that no one is going to the expense and trouble of returning a water heater. So if he's unscrupulous, he might sell you a heater with an actual life expectancy of only two years—though he, in effect, has assured you it should last for ten years.

Whether the guarantee covers the entire product or only certain parts. For example, a lifetime guarantee on a washing-machine tub covers the tub only—not the entire washer.

The reputation of the firm making the guarantee. After all, what good is a fifteen-year guarantee on a miraculous new roof coating if the firm selling the coating carefully arranges to go out of business before the coating fails in five years? None. Yet the building industry has more than its share of such dead-beat organizations.

And now for a close look at the relative merits and demerits of the most important materials, equipment and furnishings that go into the home:

AIR CONDITIONERS

Requirements. Operate reliably and efficiently with little attention; long-lasting; do not require refinishing.

Types available. Central and room air conditioners. Both types available for cooling only or, as heat pumps, for year-round heating and cooling.

Choice. Air conditioners providing cooling only require less upkeep than heat pumps, which are considerably more complicated. But between central and room air conditioners there is little choice unless you install two or three of the latter. In that case, simply because of their greater numbers, the room units are almost certain to require more attention. Since they are exposed to view, they may also require refinishing.

Among the various types of central conditioners available, those with two small condensing units (rather than one large condensing unit) are first choice.

AWNINGS

Requirements. Resist soiling; long-lasting; easy to clean.

Types available. Canvas; fiberglass; enameled aluminum.

Choice. Fiberglass first; aluminum second; canvas a dismal third. In selecting awnings of rigid material, note that those made with vertical strips, or panels, collect less dirt and are easier to clean than those with horizontal strips.

BASEMENT BULKHEADS

Used to cover outside steps into a basement.

Requirements. Do not leak; do not deteriorate; doors easy to open.

49

Types available. Prefabricated-steel bulkheads; wood bulkheads built at the site.

Choice. Steel, by all means—though it needs to be repainted often to keep it from rusting.

CABINETS, KITCHEN

Requirements. Do not show fingerprints; easy to clean outside and in; never need refinishing; shelves do not collect dust or warp; drawers do not stick or jam; doors do not warp or sag, and open and close easily.

Types available. Wood cabinets which are finished by the manufacturer or in the home; steel cabinets with baked-enamel finish; steel cabinets with wood doors; cabinets made of wood covered with laminated plastic.

Choice. The Schulers went from steel to wood to plastic, and the plastic has our resounding vote for one simple reason: Any marks made on the surface wipe right off with a damp sponge. Refinishing is never necessary.

This is not true of steel or wood, for no matter how tough the finish that a factory applies (a factory finish is much better than one applied in the home), it is eventually damaged by skin oils, diamond rings, pots and pans, acids, cleansers, etc.

Except for this, however, the only real difference between top-quality plastic, wood and metal cabinets is in the shelving. Given a choice between a solid shelf—even an easy-to-clean plastic shelf—and one of stainless-steel wire, take the latter: it almost never needs cleaning.

CARPETS

Requirements. Resist wear; resist soiling and staining; easy to clean; don't show soil; don't mat; mothproof.

Types available. Acrylic; cotton; nylon; polyester; polypropylene; rayon; wool.

Choice. If expense is no object, your first choice—at least for living rooms, dining rooms and halls—is an authentic Oriental rug made of wool.

If you can't go that high, a good grade of ordinary wool

carpet is best for adults' bedrooms. It is also best for living rooms and studies that are not regularly crisscrossed along one path by people moving about the house. Wool has more resilience than other carpet fibers and is slower to soil and to show soil. It also has good durability. But it is harder to clean; and it attracts moths (though it can be—and should be—permanently mothproofed). These qualities make it ideal for rooms which do not get very heavy use and in which spillage of liquids, etc., is rare.

In rooms that do get heavy use, nylon followed closely by acrylic are preferred because they have superior wearability; and while they soil more readily than wool, they resist staining and clean more easily. They are completely mothproof. Use them in the dining room, halls, children's rooms and the family room.

In kitchens use acrylic carpet (see floors, kitchen). Cotton is excellent in bathrooms, for although it soils rapidly, it is very easily washed.

Note. The life of all carpets is lengthened by laying them over rug cushions—preferably those made of rubber. Because these have greater resiliency than other kinds of cushion, they tend to reduce wear on carpets to a greater degree. They do not soak up liquids which penetrate through carpet; consequently they themselves do not become smelly and require cleaning (which is impossible with felt underlays). Furthermore, they protect the floor underneath from moisture. And they do not fray, ravel or create dust.

CALKING COMPOUNDS

Used to stop water and air leaks through joints in exterior walls, around doors and windows, between terraces and walks, around tub rims, in wood gutters, etc.

Requirements. Stay flexible; stick tight; resist shrinking; resist the elements.

Types available. Silicone rubber; polysulfide rubber; acrylic latex; latex; butyl rubber; oil-base.

Choice. Silicone rubber or polysulfide rubber are the only choices even though they are quite expensive. The other compounds are not in the same league. Both calks can be used to bond almost all building materials and will last for a decade or longer without attention. The only possible drawback is that some silicone rubber calks cannot be painted over.

CEILINGS

Requirements. Stay smooth, sound and flat; easy to clean.

Types available. Plaster; gypsum board; insulating board; acoustical and non-acoustical ceiling tile.

Choice. Ceiling tile with a factory finish to make it washable is as easy to clean as the other materials and does not crack like plaster or pop nails like gypsum board and insulating board. Furthermore, if the roof or pipes above the ceiling should leak, small tiles can be replaced more easily than large, unbroken expanses can be repaired.

CLOSET SHELVES AND RODS

Requirements. Not readily soiled or scarred; easy to refinish; do not sag.

Types available. Wood shelves and rods finished in the home; steel shelves with baked-enamel finish; stainless-steel rods.

Choice. Steel shelves and rods. But note that steel rods over six feet long will sag under a heavy weight and therefore need to be supported in the middle like wood rods.

CURTAINS AND DRAPERIES

Requirements. Do not deteriorate as a result of exposure to sunlight; resist fading; not damaged by heat from radiators; resist soiling; easy to clean.

Types available. You can make curtains and draperies out of almost any flexible material.

Choice. Fiberglass meets all requirements better than any other material. What's more, curtains made of it need not be lined.

The best fiberglass for curtains is Beta cloth woven from exceptionally fine glass fibers which have extra flexibility, strength and durability (you can wash Beta cloth seven times more often than ordinary fiberglass fabric). In addition, the cloth cannot burn.

Recently fiberglass's natural resistance to soil has been greatly increased by the development by Burlington Industries of a new factory-applied finish called DSR (dry soil resistance). No matter how much dry dirt and dust collect on treated curtains, you can get them sparkling clean simply by brushing.

DISHWASHERS

Requirements. Operate efficiently for ten years with a minimum of servicing; do not contribute to the deterioration of other parts of the house.

Types available. Built-in and portable models.

Choice. Although built-ins and portables made by the same manufacturer are, as a rule, almost identical in construction and operation, the portables will generally require somewhat more servicing simply because they are portable: Since the hoses and electric cord must be plugged in and unplugged every time the dishwasher is rolled out for use, they are subjected to wear and may break and need replacement long before the dishwasher reaches the end of its days.

In addition, when you roll a portable from its storage niche to the sink and back again, you subject the floor to heavy wear; you make floor cleaning and waxing that much more difficult; and you may occasionally damage kitchen cabinets and appliances—not to mention the dishwasher itself—when you bang the dishwasher into them.

In short, built-in dishwashers are first choice.

DOORS, EXTERIOR

Requirements. Close tight without sticking or binding; operate easily; do not show soil or scars; can be cleaned and refinished easily.

Types available. Conventional doors made of wood, steel, fiberglass or urethane—of paneled or flush design. Conventional doors made with a large sheet of tempered glass set in a wood or metal frame. Dutch doors made of wood in a paneled design. French doors usually resembling small-paned casement windows.

Choice. Dutch and French doors are used mainly for esthetic reasons in entrances opening onto gardens and terraces. Because Dutch doors are made in two horizontal pieces and French doors in two vertical pieces, ordinary maintenance problems associated with hinged doors are doubled; and if either half of either door becomes warped or swollen, it affects the operation of its companion half. Dirt and dust find many lodging places on the doors' paneled surfaces. Furthermore, since French doors open out rather than in, both the interior and exterior are exposed to weathering—which means extra maintenance.

Among conventional doors, those made of steel need the least upkeep as long as you do not own a big dog that scratches to come in. In this case, the only way you can prevent corrosion is to keep a paintbrush handy at all times. But without a dog, you have few worries, because steel doors do not warp, swell or contract; and they have a baked-on finish that is easy to clean and durable.

Fiberglass and urethane doors should be even better because they never under any circumstances need refinishing. But they are so new that their durability and performance have not been tested adequately.

Wood doors do not show soil any faster than other solid doors of similar design; but the finish, which is applied in the home, does not withstand washing as well as a factory finish. This means the doors must be refinished fairly frequently. And they also need attention because they change shape and size to some extent.

Whether made of wood, steel, fiberglass or urethane, flush doors do not need to be cleaned so often as paneled doors because they are free of joints and ledges on which air-borne dirt will land. You may, however, be more conscious of fingermarks on them.

The advantages and disadvantages of glass doors are covered under doors, interior.

Note. Doors with small panes of glass require more maintenance than solid doors for the obvious reasons that the panes need frequent washing and are occasionally broken.

DOORS, GARAGE

Requirements. Do not decay or corrode; operate easily; shed dirt; easy to refinish.

Types available. Sectional doors with curved tracks; one-piece doors mounted on tracks; one-piece doors mounted at the jambs; one-piece canopy-type doors. Any of these may be made of plywood, hardboard, steel, aluminum, or fiberglass.

Choice. One-piece canopy-type doors and one-piece doors mounted on tracks are the first choice from an operational standpoint. Sectional doors are least desirable.

Preferred materials are, in descending order, fiberglass, aluminum, steel, hardboard and plywood. Any lumber used in a garage door must be treated at the mill with wood preservative.

Smooth-surfaced flush doors shed dirt better than paneled doors.

DOORS, INTERIOR

Requirements. Operate easily; do not stick or bind; close as securely as the situation requires; do not show soil; do not scar; easy to clean and refinish.

Types available. Hinged, swinging, sliding and bifold doors made of wood, plywood or flakeboard finished in the home; steel with baked-on finish; urethane; and glass. (Not all types of doors are actually available in all these materials, but they can be made of them.) The doors are either paneled (i.e., with insets), flush (completely smooth) or louvered.

Also available are folding doors made of long, narrow, vertical strips of wood or metal; and accordion doors made of heavy vinyl fabric on a steel frame.

Choice. Unlike most other parts of a house, doors have a very active role to play. They let you move from one space to another. They close off spaces. They may get in your way when you don't want them to. They move and damage walls, furniture, etc. For these reasons, you cannot possibly allow the question of maintenance to rule your selection of doors. On the other hand, because doors require considerable maintenance, you cannot ignore the question.

Let's dispose first of folding and accordion doors. They require more maintenance than other doors because they have many more moving parts, any one of which can give trouble. Like sliding and bifold doors, they may also get jammed in their ceiling tracks. But warping is a problem only with folding doors with wide wood slats. Scarring is unusual, because if the doors are struck, they give with the blow. Soiling is no worse than for other doors, and actually shows up less because the surfaces are strongly contoured.

All other types of door require maintenance either because they are soiled or scarred or have twisted out of shape. But the amount of maintenance required varies with the type of door, the material of which it is made and its surface contours. How they rank from the best down is shown on the page opposite (there is no difference between doors in brackets):

Additional comment is in order:

1. I confess to being extremely allergic to louvered doors, for no matter what they are made of, they collect much dust and are hard to clean. And louvered doors made of wood are frightful to refinish.

2. Steel doors rank high as long as their original factory finish holds up. But when this eventually deteriorates from chipping, scratching and skin oils, it needs to be renewed. The work involved is no more difficult than the application of enamel to wood if you are willing to settle for the effect of painted wood. But because most people want to achieve a new finish that is as tough and flawless as the original, they must go to the trouble of spraying on new enamel.

3. The high ranking given glass doors is based on the premise that the doors are either made of very thick glass that requires no framing or have very narrow aluminum or steel frames. On a glass door with a wood frame, the frame is usually so wide that you touch the wood rather than the glass when you open or close the door. This kind of glass door must, therefore, be rated the same as a wood door.

4. Glass doors with translucent or frosted glass show soiling by hands less than those with clear glass.

5. When doors are made of large sheets of glass—as in

SOILING BY HANDS	SOILING BY AIR-BORNE DIRT	SCARRING	WARPING	EASE OF REFINISHING	EASE OF CLEANING
According to the type of door					
Sliding	No difference	Sliding	Swinging	No difference	No difference
Bifold		Bifold	Bifold		
Hinged		Swinging	Sliding		
Swinging		Hinged	Hinged		
According to material					
(Flakeboard)	No difference	Glass	(Glass)	(Glass)	Urethane
(Plywood)		Steel	(Steel)	(Urethane)	Steel
(Steel)		Urethane	(Urethane)		Glass
(Urethane)		(Wood)	Flakeboard	(Wood)	(Wood)
(Wood)		(Plywood)	Wood	(Plywood)	(Plywood)
Glass		(Flakeboard)	Plywood	(Flakeboard)	(Flakeboard)
				Steel	
According to surface contours					
Paneled	Flush	Louvered	No difference	Flush	Flush
Louvered	Louvered	Paneled		Paneled	Paneled
Flush	Paneled	Flush		Louvered	Louvered

sliding terrace doors—the glass used must either be tempered or reinforced with plastic or wire. The former is the more common.

6. The low rating given hinged doors ignores a point in their favor: The hinges on which they hang rarely give any trouble. By contrast, sliding doors often jump out of their tracks; bifold doors sometimes bind in their tracks; and the spring hinge controlling swinging doors often needs lubrication and cleaning and occasionally pulls loose from the floor.

On the other hand, hinged doors have troublemaking latches while the others do not.

7. Flush wood doors can be made highly resistant to scarring and much easier to clean if they are covered on both sides with sheets of laminated plastic.

8. While any interior door made of wood may warp, flush doors with a solid core are generally the most warp-resistant.

9. Regardless of the type of wood door used, your best assurance that it will not warp is to buy a quality door built to the standards of the National Woodwork Manufacturers Association. Many doors are also guaranteed by the manufacturer provided that your builder handles them properly. What this means is that the doors must be stored only in a dry, protected place—not in a damp warehouse or newly plastered room. They must not be exposed to unusual heat or dryness. They must be stored flat on level supports—not stood on edge or on end. The top door must be covered. And the top and bottom edges of each door must be painted or varnished after trimming and before the doors are hung.

DOORS, SLIDING GLASS

Used mainly to divide interior areas from terraces.

Requirement. Work easily; do not bind; remain in their tracks; keep out the weather; easy to clean; do not require refinishing.

Types available. Doors with aluminum frames, wood frames or vinyl-clad wood frames.

Choice. Wood-framed doors must be refinished from time to time; and since they do not enjoy any unique advantages from the maintenance standpoint, there is no point in using them.

Door with aluminum frames and vinyl-clad frames are on a par. This assumes, of course, that you buy doors of equal—and, I hope, top—quality.

Here are some of the important earmarks of a good door that will require little maintenance:

It is equipped with safety glass. Stationary panels alongside are also equipped with safety glass.

It operates smoothly but takes a little effort on your part. This is an indication that it is well weather-stripped and will not leak water or air.

The sliding screen is rigid and secure in its track.

The sill track slopes outward to give added protection against water and dirt infiltration. The sill should also be recessed sufficiently into the floor so you won't trip over it.

Aluminum doors should bear the Quality Certified label of the Architectural Aluminum Manufacturers Association.

Note. Adding safety bars at door-handle level helps to keep hands from smudging the glass and also keeps people from banging into the glass. The bars can be installed on only one side of a door.

EXTERIOR-TRIM FINISHES

Requirements. Resist scarring, flaking, blistering, alligatoring, chalking, etc.; slow to fade; long-lasting; clean easily; protect the trim against cracking and decay.

Types available. Trim and shutter enamel; varnish; no finish at all.

Choice. You can reduce maintenance by not using a finish provided the trim is thoroughly treated with a wood preservative and water repellent. Such treatment is particularly important on horizontal surfaces that do not readily shed moisture—window sills, porch railings, etc.

Trim and shutter enamel is more durable than varnish and just as easily cleaned, but shows soil to a greater extent. If you use varnish, buy one containing urethane.

EXTERIOR WALLS

Requirements. Keep out the weather; do not crack; resist damage by falling tree limbs, ladders, etc.; shed dirt; easy to clean; need little or no refinishing.

Types available. Prefinished aluminum; asbestos-cement; asphalt shingles and roll siding; brick; nail-on brick; molded brick and stone; concrete block; prefinished fiberboard; unfinished and prefinished hardboard; unfinished and prefinished plywood; stone; stucco; vinyl; wood; shingles and shakes.

Choice. Several of these materials can be eliminated at the outset: Nail-on brick and molded brick and stone, because the joints may crack open if there is any movement in the framework of the house. Stucco, which tends to crack with the settlement of the house. Fiberboard, because it is easily damaged. Asphalt shingles and roll siding, because they can also be damaged and gradually lose their mineral surface.

Several other materials should be avoided if you are thinking of applying paint, stain or a clear finish to them. These include unfinished hardboard, unfinished plywood, wood, wood shingles and shakes, brick and concrete block. On the other hand, if you use prefinished hardboard or plywood or if you do not apply any finish to wood, wood shingles and shakes, brick and concrete block, the every four-to-six-year problem of refinishing the house can almost be forgotten.

If you add to this list of six materials, the other materials that I haven't discussed, you can see that the available selection of easy-to-maintain sidings is very broad indeed. Here are the points to consider when choosing between them:

Stone is used only on new houses and new additions. It is the most expensive siding material, in large part because it is difficult to work with. Furthermore, there are relatively few masons today who are skilled in handling it; and if you happen to employ a man who is unskilled, you are likely to wind up with walls that leak, effloresce or require painting. Another possible drawback of stone walls is the fact that their rough surface traps dirt and holds it rather stubbornly even under a stream of water. On the other side of the coin, however, you usually cannot see dirt on stone as clearly as on smoother surfaces. And when a stone wall is well built, it lasts forever and never needs attention.

Brick is also a costly siding which is used only on new houses and additions. It may also leak, effloresce and need repainting if you employ sloppy workmen. But when well built, a brick wall is extremely durable and rarely needs washing except in very sooty cities. (*Note:* Used brick should never be used in exterior walls because it is much less durable than new brick and may develop leaks.)

Vinyl is moderately expensive at the moment, although if it continues to grow in popularity, the price should drop. It is used on new and old homes. Because it has been available for only a few years, little is known about its durability and whether it will develop problems. But to date it has performed very well and holds promise of being one of the most maintenance-free materials available. It soils grudgingly; washes easily. It does not warp or dent, though it can be broken by a hard blow. Because it is solid color throughout, it never needs to be painted, does not blister or peel, and does not show scratches.

Prefinished aluminum siding is also moderately expensive; goes on new houses and old. Its durability and cleanability have been tested by more than a decade of use. Many manufacturers now guarantee the finishes applied to the metal panels for twenty years or more. Nevertheless, installers who handle both aluminum and vinyl rate the vinyl slightly higher. Reason: The finish of aluminum can be damaged; the metal itself can be dented.

Prefinished steel siding is similar to aluminum in all respects. One plus: It is stronger and more rigid. A minus: The steel will rust if the finish is scratched.

Plywood is a medium-cost material used mainly in new construction, though it can be used for residing. It meets all the requirements for easy maintenance. In fact, you never have to give it a thought. One of its plus values is the fact that it adds extra strength and stiffness to the structure of a house and greatly helps to protect it against hurricanes, earthquakes and earth slides. Plywood that is finished at the factory with a polyvinyl-chloride film is guaranteed by many manufacturers never to need painting. Unfinished textured plywoods that are allowed to weather naturally do not require attention either (because of their slight roughness, however, they shed dirt a little less easily than prefinished plywood).

Prefinished hardboard has the same easy-maintenance properties as prefinished plywood. However, no manufacturer has yet guaranteed the finish for the life of the house. Hardboard also lacks the exceptional strength of plywood. On the other hand, it is more resistant to moisture and termites.

Wood and wood shingles and shakes are medium-cost materials used mainly in new homes. Shingles are also used for residing. If allowed to weather naturally, they demand little attention. Wood boards, however, sometimes split or cup. And because shingles and shakes are rough textured, they slowly collect dirt and are reluctant to give it up except when hosed down hard.

Asbestos-cement sheets are a low-cost siding material; shingles and clapboards of the same material are a bit more expensive. All are tough, fire-resistant and long-lasting. Their only fault is that they can be shattered by a hard blow. The sheets are almost as smooth as glass and shed air-borne dirt but hand-smudge badly. If you like their natural slate-gray color, they don't need painting; otherwise they must be repainted every four to six years. Shingles and shakes have a long-life plastic finish in various colors and a slight texture that tends to trap dirt after a period of time.

Concrete block is of medium cost. If you don't paint it, upkeep is easy. But an occasional hosing down is in order. A special advantage of solid-block walls (not veneered walls) is that they turn away termites and hurricane-force winds. This is why they are so often used in Florida and similar areas.

EXTERIOR WALL FINISHES APPLIED AT THE SITE

Requirements. Resist flaking, blistering, alligatoring, etc.;

long-lasting; slow to fade; shed dirt and wash easily; do not mildew; easy to apply.

Types available. Latex, oil and Portland cement paints; penetrating and opaque stains; bleaches; penetrating sealer; linseed oil; processed resin-free oil; varnish; no finish at all.

Choice. While a finish changes the appearance of an exterior wall, it does not protect or extend the life of siding materials such as wood, plywood, brick, stone, concrete block or stucco. Nor does it necessarily improve the wall's ability to shed dirt. It follows that if you want to save work and expense, you should not apply any finish to your walls. Just let them weather. Wood boards may sometimes cup or split, but neither action is inevitable.

The speed with which the weathering process changes the appearance of a wall varies with the material, exposure, climate, etc. Masonry walls usually show little change except in dirty cities and in the event that they effloresce. (They would change in the same circumstances if painted.) Wood and plywood walls change more rapidly, although unevenly, so it may take several years to complete the process. This can be speeded up, however, by applying one coat of bleach to the new wood. Additional applications should not be necessary because, by the time the bleach "wears out," the wood will have weathered naturally.

In the case of redwood, the California Redwood Association recommends the application of a water repellent to modify the natural bleaching process so that the wood will arrive at a desirable light-tan color without going through undesirable darkening stages. In humid climates, a mildewcide should be added to the repellent.

Whatever the claims made for them, other types of clear finishes need to be renewed frequently. Walls coated with linseed oil also collect dirt and mildew.

Opaque, pigmented stains on wood require less maintenance than paint because they do not crack, craze and blister, and have less tendency to peel. They last longer. And when they are renewed, the work is easier because you can get by with less surface preparation and need to apply only one coat.

63

Opaque stains are particularly desirable on rough wood because they penetrate the pores of all surfaces and wear evenly. Paint, on the other hand, does not penetrate. During application, it tends to run off the ridges of the wood into the valleys; as a result, the thinner coat on the ridges wears away long before the thicker coat in the valleys.

On masonry walls, exterior latex paint performs better than anything else. It is also slightly better than oil paint on wood walls—especially on new cedar. This is because cedar sometimes exudes tannic acid which stains oil paint and oil stain but which does not affect latex paint.

Other advantages of latex paint are: (1) It allows most of the moisture in the wall to escape; consequently there is little or no blistering and peeling as with oil paint. (2) It is easier to apply than oil paint and can be applied to damp surfaces. (3) It dries so very rapidly that you can, if necessary, apply two coats in one day. This may save a lot of ladder-moving.

On the other hand, you must take greater pains in preparing the surface for latex paint.

Both latex and oil paint are available in one-coat formulations; but only the best of these are guaranteed to give one-coat coverage—and that guarantee is based on the assumption that you are applying the paint over a previously finished surface that is in sound condition. In other words, one-coat house paint may or may not save you work when you repaint your house. While it will last somewhat longer than a single coat of ordinary paint and resist fading better because of its high pigment content, it will not outlast two coats of ordinary paint. And in between paint jobs, it will require just as much cleaning and other maintenance as ordinary paint.

Note. Don't under any circumstances paint your house with one of the so-called protective coatings which are said not only to provide a beautiful, everlasting finish but also to stop dampness, retard fire, absorb noise, cut fuel bills, etc. These are dishonest products which in the end will cause you more trouble and expense than even the cheapest conventional paint.

A good example of how not to paint a house. The carpenter used ordinary steel nails rather than galvanized. These rusted before the painters got around to puttying over the heads with the result that the rust stains bled through the putty and the finish. To make matters worse, the painters concocted their own opaque stain out of paint and turpentine instead of using a ready-made stain containing penetrating oils. As a result, the finish did not penetrate into the pores of the wood and began to flake off within a few months.

FENCES

Requirements. Do not need painting; resist damage; remain upright.

Types available. Wood; steel; plastic panels in a wood frame.

Choice. A post-and-rail fence with posts that are pressure treated with wood preservative is probably the most durable and maintenance-free fence you can erect. But any unfinished wood fence with pressure-treated posts is good provided that wide horizontal members are sloped slightly to one side so that water will drain off rapidly and provided also that pickets or rails, which extend within a few inches of the ground, are treated at that point with preservative. Of course, the more nearly solid a painted wood fence, the more it gets splattered with dirt and the more frequently it needs cleaning and repainting.

Steel fences are undeniably strong—perhaps too strong because if hit by a car they will bend rather than break like a wood fence and will be extremely hard to repair. But their principal problem is that, no matter how well galvanized they are when new, they eventually begin to rust. Repainting is extremely difficult.

Fences built with large plastic panels set in an unfinished wood frame with pressure-treated posts need no refinishing and remain upright as well as any fence. But the plastic cannot withstand very hard blows.

FLASHING

Used to prevent leaks in roof valleys, around chimneys, over doors and windows, etc.

Requirements. Does not develop holes for any reason; does not corrode and stain surfaces below.

Types available. Copper; aluminum; galvanized iron; asphalt roll roofing.

Choice. Copper is expensive but far and away the best: Once installed, you can forget about it. True, it may stain adjacent surfaces green; but as a rule, flashing is installed in places where any staining it causes will not be seen.

Aluminum is an inexpensive second choice. If in contact with masonry, it must be thoroughly painted with an alkali-resistant coating to prevent rapid corrosion.

FLOORS LAID ON ON-GRADE AND BELOW-GRADE CONCRETE SLABS

Requirements. Not damaged or loosened by the moisture and alkalies in the concrete; wear well under traffic; do not dent; don't fade; resist soiling and staining; easy to clean and keep attractive; mildewproof.

Types available. Solid vinyl; vinyl-asbestos; asphalt tile; rubber tile; seamless flooring; mildew-resistant carpet; ceramic and quarry tile; brick; flagstone; slate; terrazzo; wood strips laid on sleepers; laminated wood blocks.

Choice. Concrete in contact with the ground is never completely dry and may therefore damage a number of common flooring materials. All the materials listed here, however, will perform satisfactorily on on-grade slabs. On below-grade slabs, laminated wood blocks and certain seamless flooring materials should not be used.

Your actual choice of material depends mainly on what the room is used for. For the advantages and disadvantages of the materials, see the entries following.

FLOORS, BATHROOM

Requirements. Must be watertight; resist staining; easy to clean.

Types available. Ceramic tile; solid vinyl; printed vinyl; linoleum; seamless flooring; carpet.

Choice. Vinyl or linoleum in sheet form to eliminate or minimize seams which may leak and catch dirt. Seamless floors that are poured from a can are equally good.

Wall-to-wall bathroom carpet made of cotton or acrylic is excellent because when it becomes soiled, you can take it up and wash it or send it to a laundry. But this adds considerably to your maintenance bill. Furthermore, the carpet is not watertight and must therefore be laid over a floor that is.

67

Ceramic tile is the most difficult to clean because dirt lodges in the joints and may stain the grout if it is not made with epoxy.

FLOORS, KITCHEN

Requirements. Long-lasting; wear well under traffic; resist soiling, scratching, indentation; not damaged by grease, alkalies, acids; do not stain; easy to clean and keep attractive; stay down; don't fade; reduce breakage.

Types available. Any flooring material can be used in kitchens; but for various reasons, the materials most often used are solid vinyl; printed vinyl; vinyl-asbestos; linoleum; asphalt tile; rubber tile; seamless flooring; carpet. Sheet materials, tiles and poured, seamless materials.

Choice. Asphalt and rubber tile are not recommended for kitchens because they have rather poor resistance to grease and soil. Of the remaining resilient materials, solid vinyl— the most expensive—is the most durable and easiest to maintain. But the others come very close and cost less.

Floors covered with resilient tile have a great many more joints than those covered with resilient sheet materials and consequently collect more dirt and require more cleaning. The joints may also leak, causing the tiles to loosen. On the other hand, in the rather unlikely event that a floor is damaged, it is easier to replace a tile or two than to mend holes in a sheet material.

In the maintenance race, vinyl's toughest competition comes from the so-called seamless flooring materials. These are made by pouring plastic from a can, spreading it on the floor as if it were paint, embedding in it solid particles to give color and texture, and then covering with additional liquid plastic. The most common seamless floors are made with a liquid acrylic, polyester, urethane or epoxy—or a combination of these plastics—and plastic chips. Other seamless floors, which resemble terrazzo, are made with liquid epoxy and marble chips or ceramic granules.

Unlike vinyl and other resilient floors, all of which need to be swept, damp-mopped, washed, waxed and stripped, seamless floors have a natural glossy finish and never need waxing or stripping. But they must be reglazed when the surface becomes dull (see page 165); and like most floors, they eventually wear down in heavy-traffic areas and then need to be resurfaced. These problems are, however, minimized if you put in a urethane floor or, even better, an epoxy floor with marble or ceramic chips. Such floors have extremely good resistance to abrasion—in fact, the epoxy floors are almost as tough as clay tile.

Another maintenance advantage of seamless floors is that they are more resistant to indentation than resilient floors. (This means, however, that they are less comfortable underfoot.)

On the other hand, seamless floors are more difficult to lay than resilient floors, so there is more chance that you might get a sloppy installation that would require extra maintenance and repairs. Urethane floors also have a tendency to yellow, especially when exposed to sunlight.

Claims that carpet is easier to maintain than a smooth floor have little merit. Indoor-outdoor carpet made of polypropylene has no place in the kitchen despite some manufacturers' assertions to the contrary. Acrylic carpet is much better because it resists staining by most things used in a kitchen. But while spots wipe up easily, you must decide which of many cleaning agents to use; and if you don't choose the right one, you may make matters worse. Furthermore, when you are working in a carpeted kitchen, you don't always immediately notice that you have dropped something on the floor. Consequently the spot may set for several days before you discover it; and by then it has attracted dirt and become more difficult to clean.

This is one of the problems with carpet that you don't have with a smooth floor. Another is the fact that it wears out in traffic lanes and must be replaced about twice as often as a smooth floor.

Finally, while there is merit to the argument that because a carpet hides dirt you don't feel pushed to clean it so often, it is nevertheless true that a carpet does get dirty; and when it does, you need to haul out a vacuum cleaner to get up the embedded particles. This is a harder job than wielding a broom. And shampooing a carpet—as should be done two or three times a year in the kitchen—is no easier than stripping wax from a smooth floor.

Note. All flooring materials may fade if exposed to long hours of sunlight. This is most generally true of reds and light pastel tones. However, since each material is something of a law unto itself, you should check the point with your flooring dealer.

FLOORS—LIVING AREAS

Requirements. Wear well under traffic; resist denting, fading, staining and soil; easy to clean and keep attractive; don't squeak or creak.

Types available. Hardwood and softwood strips; hardwood blocks (parquet); solid vinyl; printed vinyl; vinyl-asbestos; asphalt tile; rubber tile; seamless flooring; brick; quarry tile; slate; flagstone; marble; terrazzo.

Choice. Quarry tile must be swept or vacuumed and damp-mopped occasionally. That's all the maintenance it requires. In short, it is a nearly perfect flooring material from the standpoint of upkeep. But because it is cold and hard, it is a material you are not likely to use except in entry halls, sun-rooms and around indoor swimming pools.

The other hard flooring materials are usually used in the same limited ways. All are somewhat more difficult to care for.

In the first year after it is laid, terrazzo needs considerable attention in order to seal the pores and prevent dusting; but much of this work should be the responsibility of the contractor. Thereafter, the floor needs only to be swept, mopped and occasionally given a scrubbing and buffing. It also needs to be resealed.

Brick should be sealed with a solvent-based silicone sealer and should then be kept waxed so that stains will not penetrate and traffic will not scuff off a fine, abrasive dust. Cleaning of brick—and also flagstone and slate—is complicated to

70

some extent by the slight roughness of the surface: even with a good vacuum, it is sometimes difficult to lift off lint.

Marble scratches readily and is etched by acids; so it must be rehoned by a contractor now and then. Routine care calls for sweeping and damp-mopping, and application of a penetrating sealer three or four times a year.

Outside the kitchen and bathrooms, resilient and seamless flooring are generally limited to entry halls and family rooms. In entries they are desirable because they are not fazed by the water and snow that are tracked in, and they are easily cleaned and mopped. But as in kitchens, the resilient materials do need to be waxed and stripped; the seamless floors must occasionally by reglazed.

In family rooms, seamless flooring is a good choice because of its easy cleanability and its excellent resistance to abrasion and indentation. But you may feel that its lack of resilience is a mark against it. Before selecting a resilient floor in preference, however, you should note that all resilient materials are dented rather badly by static loads (chairs, tables, pianos, etc.) and by dynamic loads (heels and other sharp blows); and there is no sure way to stop this. The best you can do is to use a solid vinyl backed by a foamed vinyl in a room in which extensive damage by heels and blows is anticipated; and use a solid, unbacked vinyl in a room with very heavy furniture. Both materials have unusually good ability to return to their original shape when subjected to heavy loads; but whereas the cushioned vinyl has better resistance to dynamic loads, the solid, homogeneous vinyl has better resistance to static loads.

Other ways suggested by the Armstrong Cork Company to minimize or conceal dents in resilient floors include the following: Use light, multicolored materials rather than dark solids. Use materials with random designs—swirls, marblelike grainings, spatterdash mottling, etc. Use textured materials. Apply low-gloss wax to minimize shadows made by dents.

In living rooms, dining rooms and bedrooms, wood and carpet have traditionally been favorite materials; and although neither come close to being ideal low-upkeep materials, I doubt if you are about to break tradition. You can, however, make efforts to use the wood and carpet which will require least attention over a long period of time.

We can eliminate softwood floors at the outset: They wear very badly. Oak is the best of the hardwoods, not so much because of its durability but because it has a stronger grain than maple, beech and birch and therefore does not show scratches and other blemishes so clearly.

The outstanding oak flooring is a parquet block which is impregnated with a plastic. The manufacturer claims it is then "hardened by exposure to nuclear radiation." The wood is extremely hard, resistant to abrasion, indentation, heat and staining. No finish or wax are used. Normal maintenance consists of cleaning with an oil-treated mop or damp mop, and occasionally light buffing. Deep scratches are removed by sanding followed by a little buffing to return the surface to its original appearance. Although the blocks' original cost is high, they last so long and require so little maintenance that their amortized cost is low.

All other hardwood flooring should be coated with a hard finish and then waxed. Thereafter, unless it is exposed to hard wear or excessive moisture (either standing water or, worse, persistent high humidity), it should need only routine dusting, occasional buffing and a very occasional waxing. In an old house, you may also have to do something now and then about boards that creak. (This is one advantage that any kind of wood block has over wood strips: creaking is rarely a problem. On the other hand, blocks are much more difficult to refinish.)

No carpet measures up to a hardwood floor in durability or ease of maintenance. Even the best—a fine Oriental rug— eventually becomes worn enough to merit replacement. And even the best mildewproof and mothproof nylon or acrylic carpet can become stained, dented and faded, and needs to be vacuumed and shampooed.

Yet the surprising truth is this: Given a choice between a wall-to-wall carpet and a large room-size rug with a surrounding fringe of polished hardwood, you will do better with the former. There are several reasons: (1) It is more of a nuisance to clean two different flooring materials with two different cleaning tools than it is to clean one material with one cleaning tool. (2) When the wood needs to be buffed or waxed, it is a special nuisance to move out the furniture, turn back the rug and clean under its edges. (3) There is not enough difference in size between wall-to-wall carpet and a room-size rug to add appreciably to your staining and snagging problems. (4) Though a wall-to-wall carpet wears out over a somewhat larger area than a room-size rug, it does not need replacement any sooner. (5) True, wall-to-wall carpet costs more initially and costs more every time you have it professionally cleaned. But remember that this added cost is reduced slightly by the cost of buffing, waxing, and perhaps refinishing the wood.

The only time when wall-to-wall carpet loses its maintenance advantage to a rug is when the area of the rug is smaller than the area of the exposed hardwood.

FLOOR FINISHES

Requirement. Protect the surface underneath; resist wear; do not yellow; easy to clean and keep attractive.

Types available. Floor varnish; urethane varnish; penetrating seal; gym seal; shellac; stain wax; paint; plastic—all applied in the home. Prefinished wood flooring.

Choice. No finish is applied to seamless flooring or tile. Terrazzo and marble are treated every few months with a special penetrating sealer. Brick should be sealed and waxed (though this is not mandatory). Flagstone and slate may or may not be sealed and waxed. Concrete should be finished only with the epoxy paint made for the purpose.

Resilient flooring materials should never be coated with any kind of clear, hard sealer, because it will probably yellow; and when it wears off in traffic lanes, what remains can neither be removed without damage to the floor nor patched so you cannot see the edges.

Despite some claims to the contrary, however, all resilient

materials look and perform better if they are waxed. Only a water-based wax should be used. Three types are available: (1) Clean-and-polish waxes do exactly that: clean and wax the floor in one step. They are self-polishing. These are obviously the easiest of all waxes to use, but they are the least durable—which means you either must apply them more often or use them only in areas that receive light traffic. The most efficient products contain ammonia. (2) Self-polishing waxes are more durable but more troublesome because you should clean the floor well before applying them. (3) Buffable waxes are the most tedious to apply because you should clean the floor first; then after the wax is dry, you must buff it with an electric polisher to attain a full gloss. But they wear best of all.

On wood, a finish applied in the home by a professional floor finisher is better than a factory finish and more easily repaired when that becomes necessary. This assumes, of course, that the finish he applies is a good one.

The best are penetrating seal, which is moderate in cost, and urethane varnish, which is expensive. The latter is a tougher finish, withstanding more abuse and giving better protection to the wood; but it is difficult to patch without showing lines of demarcation between the old varnish and the new. Penetrating seal gives less protection to the wood and is itself more easily scratched; but the scratches can sometimes be obliterated simply by rubbing with turpentine. If that fails, rub on some more penetrating seal. It blends into the old.

My experience with penetrating seal does not convince me that it is a perfect product; but it does well enough to get my vote, especially when used on softwoods. On hardwoods, urethane varnish does just as well, but no better.

Both finishes—like all other finishes applied to wood— should be protected with wax. Because water will damage wood, use solvent-based wax only. There are three types, all of which clean at the same time that they polish: (1) Paste wax gives the toughest, longest-lasting finish; and the luster can be maintained for many months by buffing with an electric floor polisher. But you must get down on hands and knees to apply the wax. (2) Self-polishing liquid wax goes on fastest and with least effort; but it is the least durable, and when it loses its luster it must be reapplied. You thus build up a thick coating which wears unevenly and needs to be stripped long before other waxes. (3) Buffable liquid wax is, in the long run, the best to use even though you must have an electric floor polisher. The wax is of medium durability; but it can be rebuffed many times before reapplication is called for.

If paint rather than a clear finish is applied to a wood floor, use epoxy floor enamel. Nothing else will last very long. Waxing with a solvent-based wax helps to protect the finish somewhat.

Note. No household electric floor polisher is the equal of the heavy machines used by professional floor-care firms. However, of the types available, that with a single polishing disk gives the best results.

FURNITURE, METAL

Requirements. Resists corrosion and scratching; does not need refinishing; easy to clean.

Types available. Chrome-plated steel; brass-plated steel; aluminum; painted steel; wrought iron.

Choice. Aluminum, by a whisker. Wrought iron is not so easy to clean. Chrome-plated steel, though the easiest of all to clean, sometimes gets badly scratched. The other materials are least desirable because the finish soon becomes marred and repainting is required.

FURNITURE, RUSH, WICKER, RATTAN, REED

Requirements. Resists wear; will not wobble; resists soiling; easy to clean; does not require refinishing; material used does not break or unravel.

Choice. Avoid all of these: they're a headache.

FURNITURE, UPHOLSTERED

Requirements. Retains shape; seats do not sag or creak; joints remain sound; fabric does not show soil, is easy to clean and resists wear.

Types available. Too many to list.

75

Choice. The best and most comfortable upholstered furniture has coiled steel springs securely tied together and to closely spaced, meshed, fabric webbing; but, unfortunately, if the furniture is poorly constructed, the springs eventually break loose and the entire piece must be rebuilt. Furniture with flat, steel S-springs is less comfortable and less expensive; but the springs generally stay in place and the furniture therefore rarely needs rebuilding. Chairs and sofas with removable cushions for seats and backs use rubber webbing to support the seats. This may last only a few years before it sags and needs to be replaced.

Wood frames should be constructed with doweled and glued joints—not with nails or screws. Corner joints should be reinforced with wood blocks.

Padding should be made of clean cotton batting. Cushions of foam rubber outlast others. If cushions are tufted, buttons should be sewn through the filling. Welting should be cut on the bias.

The best upholstery fabric is solution-dyed and tightly woven to reduce the number and size of crevices that collect and retain dirt. "Getting dirt out of the crevices in fabric is extremely difficult and in some fabrics impossible," a leading fabric manufacturer says.

Vinyl and urethane are the most maintenance-free upholstery fabrics—if you think of them as fabrics. Among conventional fabrics, it's pretty much a toss-up between nylon and polypropylene. The former is more abrasion-resistant; the latter easier to keep clean (you can wipe it off with a damp rag). But polypropylene has good abrasion-resistance; and nylon has good cleanability.

Note. Upholstered chairs consisting of a wood or metal frame and a one-piece seat and back molded entirely out of urethane are so new that I have not included them above. But keep an eye out for them because they need very, very little upkeep. The padding and fabric are an integral part of each other. The padding, or core, is a soft, spongy urethane; the fabric, or skin, is also urethane but of a much tougher consistency. It can be made to resemble any other kind of fabric. Like vinyl, it resists abrasion and staining, can be cleaned with a damp rag.

FURNITURE, WOOD

Requirements. Will not wobble or break; resists damage by abrasion, burning, liquids, etc.; does not require refinishing; resists soiling; easy to clean.

Types available. Furniture made of solid wood, wood veneer, wood covered with laminated plastic, and urethane.

Choice. Whatever the material of which wood furniture is made, joints should be doweled and glued; and corner joints should be reinforced with blocks. Nailed and screwed furniture eventually comes apart. Hinges and other hardware should be of sturdy brass. Doors should open and close easily and precisely.

Drawers in wood furniture often require attention because they stick or come apart at the joints or because the bottoms split. To avoid trouble, look for drawers molded out of plastic. If drawers are made of wood, make certain the corners are dovetailed and reinforced with blocks. The bottoms should be of hardwood or plywood.

Assuming it is well put together, furniture made entirely of urethane is most maintenance-free. It is strong, damage-resistant, permanently finished and easy to clean with a damp rag. No wax or polish is used. Its principal drawback stems from the fact that urethane is easily molded; as a result, at this writing, urethane furniture pieces often have elaborate and complex lines—which means they collect a lot of dust.

Laminated plastic is used almost exclusively in tops of tables, chests and desks. Like kitchen counters, the tops are extremely durable and cleanable, and are even easier to keep up than urethane. But since the parts below the tops are made of wood, they are susceptible to scratching and need to be polished now and then. Furthermore, since plastic-topped furniture is rather cheap, the finish on the wood parts is less durable than that on good wood furniture.

Although many people believe solid-wood furniture is best, it actually requires just as much maintenance as veneered furniture and usually more. Veneer (plywood-surfaced on one or both sides with thin sheets of fine wood) is much more widely used in today's furniture than solid wood. One reason for this is that it is stronger and more stable dimensionally and therefore causes fewer problems that demand attention. In all other respects, the two materials are identical.

(Veneered furniture built prior to about 1950, however, was generally inferior to that made of solid wood because the glues used to hold the thin plies together frequently failed.)

Solid-wood and veneered furniture sometimes contain urethane panels or inserts. Far from making the furniture easier to maintain, the urethane usually makes life more difficult because it is elaborately sculptured and collects dust. (Carved and sculptured wood would be equally troublesome, but is virtually unknown today—except in antiques—because it is too expensive to produce.)

GARBAGE DISPOSERS

Requirements. Perform efficiently for fifteen years without servicing; do not jam.

Types available. Continuous-feed and batch-feed models.

Choice. This should not be dictated by the way food waste is fed into the disposer: one type is as durable and efficient as the other.

Probably the best way to judge the ease of maintaining a disposer is to look at the price tag. Low-cost disposers are made primarily for speculative home builders and apartment-house owners and are considerably less rugged and dependable than those selling at a high price. The latter generally contain many parts of stainless steel; and they may also be partially lined with tough, corrosion-resistant epoxy or plastic. High-priced disposers are also driven by more powerful motors.

The most jam-free disposers have cutters that swivel when they strike a peach pit or other hard object. The next best are those which automatically reverse their cutting action. Least desirable are those which can be freed only with a special wrench inserted in the bottom. See also refuse disposal devices.

GARDEN WALLS

Requirements. Do not deteriorate as a result of weathering; remain upright; do not need painting.

Types available. Brick, concrete block, cinder block and stone laid up with mortar; dry-stone walls.

Choice. If you can find a man capable of building a dry-stone wall that will not shed stones or collapse, you will have a wall that will never give you a moment's trouble (except when someone pilfers a few of your precious stones). But alas, even in eastern Connecticut, where rugged stone walls are as much a part of the landscape as the pines and oaks, such artisans— I really should call them artists—have almost disappeared. So you are reduced to building a masonry wall if you put maintenance ahead of beauty.

Of those listed, concrete- or cinder-block walls have a very slight advantage simply because they contain fewer joints which may crumble and need repointing. (I assume, of course, that all masonry walls have adequate footings to hold them upright; are properly proportioned to stand up against the wind; and are not painted.)

GUTTERS AND LEADERS

Requirements. Do not leak; do not sag or bend; do not deteriorate in appearance.

Types available. Unfinished galvanized steel; enameled galvanized steel; unfinished aluminum; enameled aluminum; copper; vinyl; wood.

Choice. In descending order; copper, enameled aluminum, wood, enameled steel, unfinished aluminum, vinyl, unfinished steel.

Copper may bend but is on the whole very strong and can be straightened if damaged. It will not corrode but it does discolor and can be unsightly if paint is accidentally slapped on it. Its very high cost, however, is a serious drawback.

Aluminum is less sturdy than other materials, and unfinished aluminum may corrode badly if exposed to salt and chemicals in the air or if allowed to fill with leaves. But enameled aluminum does not have these problems, and rarely requires refinishing.

Steel is the strongest guttering material next to wood. It is also the cheapest. But unfinished steel rusts out rapidly if you do not brush asphalt roof coating or polysulfide rubber in the trough every couple of years. The exterior must also be painted with rust-resistant paint. The obvious alternative is to use enameled steel.

Wood, despite its strength, requires attention to keep it from splitting and opening at the seams. It should be treated with a preservative before it is hung; thereafter, it is advisable to keep the trough painted with asphalt roofing compound. Joints between sections and at the ends may leak if not sealed with silicone or polysulfide rubber calking. The price is high.

Vinyl gutters and downspouts may, in time, prove to be the top choice. They are strong, rigid, will not corrode or split, retain their appearance and never need painting. At the moment, however, they are causing problems because they expand and contract rather sharply with changes in temperature. As a result, they often leak badly at the joints.

Note. Dissimilar metals should never be used together in the same gutter or leader.

HARDWARE

Used on doors, cabinets, windows, etc.

Requirements. Latches and locks work easily, resist jamming and breaking. Tracks for sliding, bifold and folding doors hold doors firmly and allow them to operate easily. All exposed hardware resists corrosion, discoloration and loss of finish.

Types available. Hardware comes in three general grades: commercial, medium and builder's, or lightweight.

Choice. The commercial grade is by far the most expensive but also by far the most durable. The medium grade gives a very good performance, however. Never buy the builder's grade, which borders on the shoddy.

Avoid hardware that is brass-plated—especially doorknobs, latches and other pieces that you touch. Solid brass is also a poor choice, for although it does not lose its finish, it needs rather frequent polishing. Best finishes are chrome steel, glass and ceramic.

Note. As a rule, the only outlets stocking all three grades of hardware are known as "builder's hardware suppliers." These may or may not sell retail, but will permit you to inspect the lines they carry. Lumberyards and hardware stores generally do not carry the commercial grade of hardware.

HEATING SYSTEMS

Requirements. Operate reliably and efficiently without attention; long-lasting; do not contribute to or aggravate house cleaning; maintain a desirable humidity in the house; do not require draining and refilling when the house is empty; do not leak water; do not require cleaning.

Types available. Warm air, hot water, steam and radiant systems fired by gas, oil or electricity.

Choice. An electric heating system using baseboard heaters and individual room thermostats lasts for many years and requires no maintenance because there are no moving parts, no pipes or ducts to fill, nothing to clean.

The electrical industry also makes much of the fact that electric heat is clean. It is; but a house heated by electricity is no cleaner inside than one heated by a modern gas or oil system. On the other hand, an electric heating system does not give off any by-products of combustion or require venting; consequently it does not pollute the outdoor air as other fuels do.

The only problem I have had with electric heat is not actually the fault of the heating system. Rather the fault lies in the fact that, in order to keep down the cost of electric heat, you must install storm sash and very thick insulation with good vapor barriers. Because of these, the humidity in bathrooms is unnaturally high and the windows need to be washed and painted frequently. This problem can, however, be corrected if you install a small ventilating fan in each bathroom.

One other possible problem with electric baseboard heaters

is that, if draperies extend down over them to the floor, they will become slightly scorched on the back sides. (There is little danger of fire.) Consequently, some homemakers hang their draperies only to the tops of the heaters. Another solution would be to make draperies of fiberglass.

Gas-fired systems are more maintenance-free than those using oil because they have fewer moving parts, and the burner does not require annual cleaning and adjustment.

Rating heating systems by type rather than by fuel—electric baseboard heating is followed, in descending order, by forced warm-air, circulating hot-water, steam, and radiant systems in which hot water is circulated through a grid of pipes buried in the floor or ceiling.

If you have a forced warm-air system, your only regular maintenance chore is to clean or replace the air filters. In addition, the blower should be checked annually, and occasionally requires an overhaul.

An indirect advantage of a warm-air system is that you can install in it an electrostatic air cleaner and humidifier. Both of these devices help to reduce upkeep in the home (see pages 36 and 38).

All heating systems using water may develop leaks (which are extremely difficult to locate and stop if you have a radiant heating coil buried in a concrete slab or plaster ceiling). To prevent freezing, they must be drained if you go away on vacation in the winter. In forced hot-water and radiant systems, the circulating pump requires an annual inspection and lubrication and occasional repairs. Radiators need to be vented periodically. In steam systems, the radiator valves must be cleaned and replaced once in a while; and you must add new boiler water every month or so unless you have an automatic water feeder.

HEATING SYSTEMS—FURNACES AND BOILERS

Requirements. Long-lasting; resist heat and corrosion.

Types available. Steel furnaces; cast-iron and steel boilers. Gas-fired and oil-fired.

Choice. Selecting a boiler is easy: A cast-iron unit is far and away more durable than a steel unit, particularly if your water is hard. It is also guaranteed for a much longer time.

Furnaces are more difficult to select because, although there are differences in quality and resulting maintenance, even an expert would have trouble identifying them. About the only thing you can go on is the reputation of the manufacturer and the heating contractor.

Oil-fired burners in furnaces and boilers should carry the Underwriters' Laboratories seal. Gas-fired burners should carry the American Gas Association emblem.

Regardless of the type of heating plant you install, you should double-check with your heating contractor to make sure he puts in a furnace or boiler that is properly sized to your house. An undersized plant makes for an uncomfortable house but maintenance of the plant is not affected. If a heating plant is oversized, however, it comes on frequently for short periods; and this constant on-again-off-again operation shortens the life of the unit.

INTERIOR WALLS

Requirements. Stay flat, smooth and flawless; do not crack, break, scar; easy to clean and refinish.

Types available. Plaster; gypsum board; insulating board; hardboard; wood paneling; decorative plywood.

Choice Except for textured plywood and textured plaster, which are hard to clean and refinish, all these materials meet requirements if they are properly installed in the first place and are not subjected to abuse thereafter. But if they are improperly installed and/or abused, there are big differences:

Hardboard is the toughest, most wear-resistant material. Its only drawback is that it may come loose and belly outward from the studs.

Plywood is the most difficult to install improperly and therefore the least likely to buckle, pop nails, open cracks, etc. It can, however, be scratched and gouged. (This, of course, is less true of hardwood plywoods than of those made with softwoods.)

Solid-wood paneling ranks a notch below plywood because

it expands and contracts more violently and sometimes opens gaping cracks. Since it is usually made of softwood, it also can be scratched and gouged quite easily.

Plaster, although sometimes considered a weak material, can take a remarkable amount of punishment without ill effects. But its propensity for cracking as a house settles makes it a high-upkeep material. One other bad point of which homeowners are usually not aware is that, as new plaster dries, the water vapor given off is taken up by the wood in the house. This causes the wood to warp and crack. A large Pittsburgh developer told me once: "I guarantee my homes for one year. During that period, plaster walls used to be indirectly responsible for more service calls than anything else in the house. That's why I gave them up even though Pittsburghers always used to insist on plaster."

Gypsum board is more easily damaged than plaster, and it does not hold nails and screws driven into it to hang pictures, towel rods, etc. as well. Both faults are attributable to the fact that gypsum board is inherently weaker than plaster; in addition, builders often use ⅜-inch panels when they should use ½-inch or thicker. Gypsum board's third fault is its tendency —if not properly installed—to pull away from the studs, thus causing the nails to pop and blister the wall surfaces.

Insulating board is the least desirable wall-surfacing material because you can gouge it and kick holes through it without even trying. Panels surfaced at the factory with a vinyl covering are somewhat stronger, however.

INTERIOR WALLS—BATHROOMS

Note. Bathroom walls are commonly surfaced with two materials: A waterproof material above the tub and behind the lavatory and perhaps on all other walls to a height of four feet; and a moisture-resistant material, such as painted plaster or gypsum board, elsewhere. This entry deals only with waterproof materials.

Requirements. Keep water from leaking into the interior of the walls; do not crack; do not stain or water spot; easily cleaned.

The packaged bathroom described on the next page is made of four large pieces of fiberglass bolted together. Tub, lavatory — everything except the toilet is molded in to simplify maintenance. (Crane Co.)

Types available. Ceramic tile; plastic tile; metal tile; plastic laminates; enameled hardboard; glass; fiberglass.

Choice. The newest idea in bathroom design is to mold walls, floor, ceiling, tub, lavatory, medicine cabinet, towel rods, paper holder and soap dishes out of one or several pieces of fiberglass. Products on the market today include a one-piece tub enclosure and a complete (except for toilet) bathroom made in three or four large sections which are bolted together. For ease of maintenance, these products are in a class by themselves because there are almost no joints or seams that can leak; curved corners wipe clean easily; painting is never required; towel rods and similar fixtures cannot loosen.

If you dislike such unconventional bathrooms (the Schulers, for instance, rejected the fiberglass tub enclosure because, much as we appreciated its cleanability, we were depressed by its appearance), you must choose between one of the other materials. I recommend laminated plastic panels which are made especially for wall surfacing. These consist of a thin, tough sheet of decorative plastic (like that used on kitchen counters) bonded to a water-resistant base of plastic foam. The panels are cemented to any smooth surface, such as gypsum board, with waterproof mastic. In a tub recess, the joints in the corners are sealed with metal moldings finished to match the plastic; the joints between the tub rim and the panels are filled with silicone calking compound. The resulting wall is watertight, crackproof, resistant to staining and scratching, and can be cleaned quickly with a damp rag.

Enameled hardboard is similar in all respects except that the enamel can be scratched and chipped and is not so stain-resistant.

Ceramic tile requires more maintenance than sheet materials because any one of its innumerable joints may crack. Furthermore, the cement in the joints often stains badly and is very difficult to clean. These problems can be minimized to some extent, however. Joints filled with an epoxy-based grout are more stain-resistant than Portland-cement-based grouts and can usually be cleaned with soap and water. To prevent cracking and subsequent leaking, tiles in tub enclosures and shower stalls should be laid in Portland cement on a base of concrete mortar. Elsewhere in the bathroom, tiles can be installed with waterproof adhesive on gypsum board, for even though cracks may develop, there is little chance that water will seep through.

"Tiles" made of opaque structural glass present the same maintenance problems as ceramic tiles, and should be installed in the same way.

Plastic and metal tiles should never be used because the joints are rarely watertight and stain readily.

INTERIOR FINISHES FOR MASONRY WALLS

Requirements. Resist scarring; do not deteriorate from exposure to oils, sun, alkalies in the wall, etc.; do not soil or show soil; readily cleaned.

Types available. Latex and oil paints; Portland cement paint; epoxy concrete enamel.

Choice. Epoxy concrete enamel. When dry, the surface resembles a glossy porcelain, and is as easy to wash as porcelain and almost as tough.

INTERIOR FINISHES FOR PLASTER, GYPSUM-BOARD AND INSULATING-BOARD WALLS

Requirements. Resist scarring; protect the material to which they are applied; do not deteriorate from exposure to sun, skin oils, etc.; do not soil or show soil; readily cleaned.

Types available. Flat, semigloss and gloss latex and alkyd paints; textured paint; wallpaper; laminated textured paper; burlap; laminated wood veneer; vinyl wallcovering.

Choice. The widespread use of vinyl wallcoverings in commercial and institutional buildings is ample evidence that they are the most durable and easily maintained finishing materials. Three types are available. Type C, the heaviest and most wear-resistant, is normally used only in corridors and other areas through which vehicles travel. Type B—medium weight —is used on walls subjected to hard wear but not wear by moving vehicles. It is as durable as homeowners need. Type

A, which weighs about a third as much as Type C, is the kind most often used in houses. It is stain-resistant, scrubbable and withstands considerable abuse and wear.

Plastic-coated wallpaper is the most maintenance-free kind of wallpaper but does not approach the solid vinyls in this respect. It shrugs off moisture and most stains; can be washed repeatedly—in some cases with powdered cleansers. It is therefore suitable for use in kitchen, bathrooms and playrooms—but only in areas where it is not exposed to abrasion and other rough wear.

All other wallpapers are washable to some degree; but don't count too much on them. They can also be stained, and wear poorly if abused.

Burlap and laminated textured papers consisting of a backing sheet of paper and a surface sheet of grass cloth, silk, cork—almost any material you can think of—are maintenance headaches. Laminated wood veneers made of very thin wood bonded to fabric are somewhat more durable, but only if they are finished with a tough, clear finish.

Textured paint scratches badly and cannot be cleaned. When it gets dirty, the only thing you can do is to paint over it.

Conventional paint scars readily. Because it is usually applied as a solid color, it shows soil more than wallpaper, which is usually patterned. And it is more inclined to fade. But paint has definite advantages. For one thing, it does not blister and it has no seams to come loose. If damaged, it can be repaired with ease. And it is inexpensive.

There used to be some question about which kind of paint was better to use on walls—alkyd or latex—but there is little argument today. Latex has always been easier to apply and to touch up; and it dries much faster. Now it has been so improved that the best flat latex paints are as stain-resistant and washable as a glossy alkyd enamel. The only advantage that the enamel enjoys is that it does not show fingermarks as much as a flat paint.

From the cleaning standpoint, latex semigloss is about on a par with alkyd semigloss.

INTERIOR FINISHES FOR WOOD, PLYWOOD,
HARDBOARD WALLS

Requirements. Resist scarring; protect the material to which they are applied; do not deteriorate from exposure to skin oils, sun, etc; do not soil or show soil; easily cleaned.

Types available. Flat, semigloss and gloss latex and alkyd paints; pigmented stain; shellac; varnish; lacquer; wax; no finish at all. Factory-applied finishes.

Choice. Finishes applied at the factory to hardboard and ply-wood are more durable and washable than any finish applied in the home. This is especially true of baked enamel. But, un-fortunately, these finishes may be marred by a careless work-man during installation of the wallboards. And when they do become chipped, scratched or gouged, an invisible touch-up job is very difficult to achieve.

By contrast, it is fairly easy to repair a scarred finish that is applied in the home. But the routine maintenance is generally more demanding.

The toughest, easiest-to-clean opaque finish is gloss alkyd paint. Semigloss paint comes next; flat paint, a very tired last.

Latex paint does not perform well on wood. Pigmented stain, which is occasionally used to bring out the grain of wood while giving it color, requires constant attention unless overcoated with clear lacquer, varnish or wax.

If you want a clear finish on wood or plywood paneling, two coats of wax perform about as well as anything—especially in areas where the walls are subjected to abuse. Admittedly, this is not a perfect finish. For one thing, if you should ever want to change the appearance of the wall, you would have a hard time removing the wax. For another thing, the wax has a tendency to sponge up dust; and it deteriorates at points where it is frequently touched.

On the other hand, when wax does get dirty, it can be washed with a mild detergent; and stubborn grime gives way to a non-metallic scouring pad. Best of all, however, scratched and worn areas can be restored to almost pristine condition simply by the application of a little more wax.

Any good solvent-based liquid or paste floor wax or stain

wax can be used. The California Redwood Association also recommends a mixture made of two pounds beeswax dissolved in one gallon hot turpentine. It advises: "Since the turpentine is highly flammable, take special care to avoid starting a fire. Heat the turpentine in a double boiler; keep the room well ventilated. Better yet, heat the preparation out of doors. The wax solution should be kept hot during application. Let the beeswax dry for forty-eight hours, then apply a coat of any prepared white wax, and polish with a soft cloth."

Hard finishes of varnish, shellac or lacquer are easier to clean than wax and more resistant to staining. But scratch marks stand out boldly. These are very difficult to repair in varnish; but are less so in lacquer and shellac because the old finish is dissolved by the new.

Using no finish at all is not recommended except on walls, ceilings, etc. which are not exposed to moisture, grease and smudging. Thus protected, a rich-looking wood such as redwood or cypress needs little care. If it does become soiled, the marks can be removed with steel wool.

For somewhat greater protection, you can spray the bare wood with a couple of coats of wallpaper lacquer. This will not alter the natural appearance of the wood but will reduce soiling and improve cleaning.

INTERIOR WOODWORK FINISHES

Used on door and window trim, baseboards, balusters, stair railings, mantels, doors, etc.

Requirements. Resist scarring; protect the material to which they are applied; are not damaged by skin oils; easily cleaned.

Types available. Gloss and semigloss alkyd paint; shellac; varnish; lacquer; wax.

Choice. The woodwork in a house gets harder wear than wood or plywood walls; but since the surfaces are smaller, refinishing is easier. This explains why the finishes recommended for woodwork differ somewhat from those for walls.

Semigloss paint is the better of the two opaque finishes, for while it is a little harder to wash, it does not chip so badly when struck a blow. It is also easier to apply.

Because of its durability, a good grade of non-yellowing interior varnish should be used for a transparent finish on most woodwork. But use urethane varnish on surfaces subject to very hard wear: stair railings, which are worn thin by abrasion and skin oils, and flat surfaces such as mantels on which your guests may set down glasses, spill drinks, etc.

KITCHEN COUNTERS

Requirements. Easy to keep clean; resist staining, scratching, burning, breaking; keep water and other spills from dripping on the floor; are not so hard as to break glasses dropped on them.

Types available. Counters made of laminated plastic, ceramic tile, stainless steel, glass-ceramic or wood.

Choice. Wood counters should be used only in small sections as chopping blocks. They are not practical otherwise.

Of the other materials, stainless steel is least desirable because it shows scratches and always looks smudgy and dirty even though it may not be.

Ceramic tile has outstanding resistance to scratches, stains and heat; but a tile counter is very difficult to keep clean because the cement joints become stained and coated with grease (particularly near the range). It may also chip or break fragile objects which are set down on it too hard. And the tiles can be cracked by very hard blows.

Glass-ceramic has the same characteristics as ceramic tile. The smallest pieces, however, are about three times the size of large tiles; consequently there are fewer joints to keep clean. Still larger pieces—up to forty-eight inches long and twenty-five inches wide—are also available.

Laminated plastic can be burned if very hot pots are placed on it. Solid colors show scratches. And occasionally the plastic separates from the plywood or chipboard base (this is particularly true of counters which are fabricated in the kitchen rather than under pressure in a mill). But as a rule, plastic-covered counters are the easiest of all to care for.

Whatever the material used, counters should incorporate backsplashes at least four inches high to protect the walls

Kitchen counters made of large, tough glass-ceramic material are easy to maintain because they are almost impervious to damage and can be wiped clean in a jiffy. (Corning Glass Works)

against splashing and to keep liquids from dripping down behind the counters. The currently popular practice of building
counters without backsplashes and then cementing matching
laminated plastic sheets or tiles to the walls all the way up to
the bottom of the wall cabinets gives even better protection
against splashing, but does not stop dripping unless pains are
taken to seal the joints between counters and walls.

To keep water, etc., from dripping off the front edges of
counters, the edges should be made with stainless-steel strips
that project a fraction of an inch above the countertop. It is
also possible to have laminated plastic counters molded with
a slightly raised lip at the front edge.

LIGHTING—BUILT-IN FIXTURES

Requirements. Easy to relamp; slow to collect dust and insects.

Types available. Too many to list.

Choice. The preceding statement is not meant to be coy,
funny or evasive. There are innumerable types of built-in lighting fixtures and all of them have some valid purpose. But as
with most things, some fixtures need more maintenance or are
more difficult to maintain than others. Here are the pros and
cons:

1. Cove lights are usually installed near the tops of walls
and are designed to direct all light upward against the ceiling. They are dirt-catchers supreme and very, very difficult to
clean.

2. Ceiling lights—whether recessed or surface-mounted—
which have diffusing panels under the bulbs collect and sil-
houette insects. They therefore require rather frequent cleaning. The problem is avoidable only if the fixtures are so tightly
constructed and installed that bugs cannot enter.

3. All fixtures should be designed to give easy, fast access
to light bulbs. Among those that don't are high-hat fixtures
which can be relamped only from the back; side lights with
chimneys so narrow you cannot get your hand into them to
screw in a bulb; recessed ceiling fixtures with diffusers which
are held in place by several nuts.

4. Any fixture mounted on two-story ceilings is, needless to say, sheer murder to relamp.

5. Many ornamental light fixtures have crevices, doodads, textured surfaces, etc. that catch dust and are difficult to clean. For instance, I once bought an adjustable hanging light which had a big, rather flat shade made of tiny slivers of wood glued together in accordion style. It drove my neat wife frantic because it seemed to attract every particle of dust in the house and was almost impossible to clean.

The most difficult fixture to keep clean, however, is an elaborate glass chandelier. Because it is supposed to sparkle, you can't help noticing the dust and grease that settle on it. But when you try to clean it—no wonder there are firms in metropolitan areas that make a business of cleaning glass chandeliers at a cost of fifty dollars up!

LIGHTING—BULBS

Requirements. Last a long time.

Types available. Incandescent bulbs; fluorescent tubes.

Choice. Fluorescent tubes will operate about seven to ten times longer than incandescent bulbs before replacement is required. That is enough reason to use them, even though they are actually a bit harder to replace than incandescents.

Two types of fluorescents are available: preheat tubes which require a starter and rapid-start tubes which operate without a starter. Since starters often fail, you should always try to put in rapid-start tubes.

It is also a good idea not to use fluorescent tubes over four feet long. Eight-footers are difficult to store, maneuver into the light fixture and then insert in their holders.

The frequency of replacing incandescent bulbs can be reduced by using bulbs filled with krypton gas. These provide 50 per cent longer life than standard incandescent bulbs, but there is no loss of light as with other kinds of long-life incandescent bulbs.

LIGHTING—LUMINOUS CEILING DIFFUSERS

Used to conceal and soften the glare of fluorescent tubes mounted on the ceiling.

Requirements. Do not sag and become warped; do not discolor or deteriorate; do not require frequent cleaning and are easy to clean when the work is necessary; will not break.

Types available. Diffusers of translucent acrylic, vinyl or glass. Partially open diffusers—grilles—made like egg crates or made out of perforated metal, plywood or hardboard.

Choice. Two types of diffuser should be bypassed: vinyl, which sags and turns yellow; and glass, which is heavy and breakable. The choice between the remaining types—all of them rigid and durable—is as complicated as the explanation of why it is complicated. The best I can do is this:

1. The biggest chore in maintaining diffusers is to clean them.

2. More dirt, including dust and insects, settle on a solid sheet of acrylic than on a grille. What's more, you can see it better.

3. In kitchens, grease deposits build up on acrylic diffusers and open grilles alike.

4. A dirty grille is infinitely harder to clean than a dirty sheet of acrylic. This is especially true of eggcrates; less true of perforated-metal grilles.

5. To reduce glare, lighting experts advise that you should never use a grille without putting some kind of diffusing material—preferably an acrylic panel—behind it.

What does all this add up to? Simply this:

If you install a luminous ceiling in the kitchen, use acrylic diffusers. True, you will have to take them down two or three times a year to clean off the dirt on the upper side. But the greasy film deposited on the bottom will be of little trouble.

Elsewhere in the house, use acrylic diffusers with any type of grille. Although you must then handle two pieces instead of one when you clean the light or replace a fluorescent tube, the grille helps to conceal the dirt and insects that settle on the diffuser and thus permit you to clean the diffuser less often.

LUMBER

Used in the basic structure of the home (sills, studs, joists, etc.); porch columns and stair stringers in contact with concrete or the ground; planters; sleepers; trellises; fence posts; piers and joists in closed-in or otherwise damp places.

Requirements. Resists decay and termites.

Types available. Redwood; cypress; and other lumber pressure-treated with wood preservative; any other lumber to which preservative is applied by brush, spray or dipping.

Choice. Pressure-treated lumber, such as fir or pine, generally outlasts even the best redwood and cypress. Tests in Mississippi have shown that whereas untreated yellow-pine posts driven into the ground have an average life of about three and a half years, pressure-treated yellow-pine posts last from twelve to twenty-three years (depending on the preservative used). By contrast, untreated cypress posts in Louisiana have an average life of ten years, while untreated redwood posts in California last about nine to twenty years.

Fir, pine and other lumber (but not cypress and redwood) which is brushed, sprayed or dipped in preservative lasts only a few years longer than the same lumber when untreated.

Preservatives containing oil, such as creosote and pentachlorophenol, are more effective than water-borne types; and are recommended for lumber exposed to the weather. But lumber treated with water-borne salts is generally preferable for indoor use and must be used if it is to be painted.

To give protection, a preservative must be applied to all surfaces that are cut or drilled. Ideally, pressure-treated lumber should be precut and predrilled before it is treated. If not, the cut and drilled surfaces must be brushed, sprayed or dipped in preservative at the building site.

MATTRESSES

Requirements. Do not develop hollows and lumps; edges are slow to break down under weight; ticking and padding do not shift.

Types available. Innerspring mattresses with cotton padding; innerspring mattresses with urethane padding; solid urethane.

Choice. Assuming that you compare mattresses of like quality, innerspring units with urethane padding (and sometimes a little cotton padding, too) last the longest without developing annoying problems. Make sure whatever innerspring mattress you buy has metal reinforcement along the sides.

OUTDOOR FURNITURE

Requirements. Must be sturdy; resists damage by sun, rain, wind, driving sand, etc.; does not require frequent refinishing; does not show soil; easy to clean.

Types available. Wood left natural or finished; painted iron and steel; chrome-plated steel; painted aluminum; rattan; wicker; reed; vinyl; glass; canvas.

Choice. First consider the extremes.

Without question, the furniture requiring least maintenance over a very long period of time is the rustic, fishing-camp kind of stuff made out of small, unpeeled, cedar logs. But who wants it?

Much more acceptable from the standpoints of comfort and appearance but quite undesirable from the standpoint of maintenance are rattan, wicker, reed and canvas furniture.

All the types remaining fall in the middle ground between good and bad. Each presents problems.

Wood—even redwood—looks well only if painted or finished with a clear sealer. Without such protection, it becomes dirty, stained, streaked; and is hard to clean. On the other hand, once it is finished, it must be refinished every year or two. Even with this protection, however, wood often splits and sometimes rots.

Iron and steel must also be painted every year; otherwise they begin to rust. Once that happens, refinishing becomes even more important and more difficult.

Chrome-plated steel is used only as the framework for chairs and tables. It water-spots rather badly but since the steel tubes are slender, the spots are not noticeable. In any case, the finish is easily cleaned. Scratches occur but can be touched up. In short, this material probably requires less maintenance than any of those in the middle ground. But the other material with which it is combined in a piece of furniture negates this advantage to some extent.

97

Aluminum with a factory-applied enamel is good as long as it is not scratched; but unfortunately it scratches about as easily as any painted metal. Moreover, because it is so light, the furniture blows over in the wind and the finish is scarred more than it should be.

Vinyl is used in seat cushions and as webbing on chairs and benches. If left in the open, it tends to acquire a black film which calls for frequent cleaning. This is a simple enough task on everything except webbing.

Plate glass used in tabletops shows dust and water spots—especially if the glass is clear. Breakage is always a problem.

PAVING—DRIVEWAYS

Requirements. Doesn't crack, break, pit; doesn't show oil and grease stains; doesn't create dust; doesn't scatter onto nearby lawn and garden areas; doesn't become choked with weeds; easy to sweep and clean; easy to clear of snow.

Types available. Concrete; asphalt; brick; stone block; gravel.

Choice. Concrete stains badly but otherwise meets all requirements if the driveway is well built. Staining can be prevented to large extent if the driveway consists of two narrow wheel strips with grass between. Air-entrained concrete should be used in cold climates because it is more resistant to frost action and the salts used to melt ice than standard concrete.

Asphalt paving of the type known as blacktop should be perfect but rarely is because paving contractors take short cuts that result in cracking and serious pitting of the surface. The only way to prevent this is to investigate the contractor's reputation carefully and to insist that he build the driveway in conformance with specifications and methods laid down by your state highway department.

A second type of asphalt paving—made by building up alternate layers of asphalt and sand—is, as a rule, less durable than blacktop because water penetrates more easily.

Brick laid in concrete is third choice, followed by brick laid on crushed stone. The former is more durable, easier to plow and doesn't sprout weeds; but the latter is easier to repair, because you can lift out a broken brick and replace it in a minute.

Stone, if cut very square, is about the equal of brick, but otherwise is more difficult to sweep and hose down. It, too, can be laid either in concrete or on crushed stone.

Gravel is completely unacceptable, although it is much the cheapest.

PAVING—TERRACES AND WALKS

Requirements. Does not crack, spall or stain; doesn't scatter onto adjoining surfaces; doesn't sprout weeds; easy to sweep and clean; drains rapidly; walks should be easy to shovel.

Types available. Concrete; coarse-aggregate concrete; brick; flagstone; stone block; quarry tile; slate; redwood and cypress blocks; seamless flooring made of epoxy with ceramic granules; indoor-outdoor carpet.

Choice. Concrete and quarry tile run a close race. Concrete is more durable and a trifle easier to sweep and hose down. Quarry tile is more stain-resistant and does not dust or hold dust so readily. For the latter reasons, I recommend tile on a terrace—especially one that is used for eating and outdoor cooking. Concrete is better for walks—in part because its rougher surface tends to remove sand and dirt from shoes before they enter the house.

Seamless flooring should be used outdoors only if the granules are resistant to ultraviolet. This is a new product and has not been in use long enough to show exactly what it can and cannot do. However, it seems to be very resistant to stains, not affected by snow-removal chemicals and easy to clean. But in time it will probably need resurfacing.

If brick, flagstone, stone block and slate are all laid in the same way—either in concrete or on sand or crushed stone—there is little to choose between them.

Coarse-aggregate concrete shows stains less than other materials—especially smooth concrete—and also removes more dirt from shoes. But it is difficult to sweep and hose down.

Wood blocks are also hard to sweep and in time need to be

replaced. In addition, like bricks that are laid in shade, they are very slippery when wet and need an occasional hard scrubbing to make them less treacherous.

Indoor-outdoor carpets made entirely of polypropylene or acrylic, and solution-dyed, will resist the fading and decomposition that plagued some of the early carpets of this type. But they do not last as long as any of the hard-surfaced paving materials. They should be taken up in winter, otherwise they will be damaged by snow shoveling. And although they can be cleaned, the work is not so easy as carpetmakers imply because as long as they are damp they cling to dirt and cannot be swept but must be hosed down; and even when dry, they can be cleaned better with a vacuum than with a broom.

PLUMBING FITTINGS (FAUCETS, SHOWER HEADS, ETC.)

Requirements. Work easily; do not clog or drip; resist wear and corrosion.

Types available. Many types, designs and qualities.

Choice. As my plumber said the other day when he came to replace a fixture: "Buy the best available; even that isn't any too good these days."

The best fittings are made of brass and bronze heavily plated with chrome. Items with fancy finishes, though commanding a higher price, are rarely as maintenance-free. Avoid ceramic knobs, which are subject to breakage.

Washerless faucets need less attention than old-fashioned types with washers. When faucet handles, drain handle and spout are mounted together in one piece, they are easier to clean around than when they are mounted separately in three or four pieces. In lavatories the spout should clear the rim of the basin enough to permit you to clean under it easily.

In hard-water areas, make sure shower heads can be taken apart easily for cleaning.

PLUMBING FIXTURES—LAVATORIES

Requirements. Clean easily; resist chipping and breakage; help to prevent water dripping onto floor.

Types available. Vitreous enamel; porcelain enamel on cast iron; porcelain enamel on steel.

Wide rims around lavatories help to contain splashing; the simple, one-piece water control is easy to clean around. Wall-hung toilet is reflected in mirror. (American Standard, Inc.)

Choice. From best to least good—in the order given above. But lavatory design must also be considered.

Whether lavatories are freestanding or built into a counter, those with large bowls and wide rims are preferable because you cannot drip and splash water out of the bowls onto the floor and surrounding walls so easily. When installed in counters, cleaning up around them is also easier. This is especially true if the rim has a shallow, built-in soap dish.

An additional disadvantage of built-in lavatories with narrow rims is that there is more chance for soap and dirt to lodge against the edges of the chrome mounting rim. If the lavatory is mounted completely under the countertop, so that the rim is not visible, soap and dirt lodge in the joint between countertop and rim.

Freestanding lavatories installed tight to the wall are preferable to those out from the wall because you do not need to clean behind them. But the difficulty of cleaning behind an out-from-the-wall lavatory can be corrected to some extent by allowing a space of at least 1½ inches—and preferably 2 inches—between the wall and the lavatory.

See also plumbing fittings.

PLUMBING FIXTURES—SHOWER STALLS

Requirements. Do not leak, especially at the base; need little cleaning; easy to clean.

Types available. Prefabricated stalls of fiberglass or steel finished in baked or porcelain enamel; ceramic tile or glass stalls built in the home.

Choice. From the maintenance standpoint, the three critical parts of a shower stall are the floor, or receptor, the walls and the door.

By all odds, the most maintenance-free stall is made of fiberglass molded in one piece to eliminate joints between walls and floor. Unfortunately, however, the models available at this time require shower curtains. These inevitably allow some water to splash onto the bathroom floor.

Another type of fiberglass shower stall has a leakproof, mildewproof fiberglass door, but because the floor and walls are joined together in the home, leaks at the base are possible, though not likely.

Leaks at the base are also possible, though unlikely, with all other types of shower stall. The most vulnerable are the porcelain-enameled steel receptors used with steel stalls. Receptors built in the home of sheet lead covered with ceramic tile are only as reliable as the workman who builds them. Prefabricated cast-stone receptors are generally the best.

Ceramic-tile walls show water spots if the tiles have a gloss finish; the mortar joints may stain badly; and cleaning is laborious. Steel walls are easier to clean but are subject to corrosion, chipping and scratching. This is particularly true of walls with baked-enamel finish.

Doors on prefabricated or home-assembled shower stalls are generally made of glass, but sometimes made of plastic. Curtains are also used but in the long run cause more trouble than doors. However, doors are far from perfect since they have an annoying tendency to leak at the bottom. Glass doors must be made of tempered glass. If translucent, they show water spots less than if transparent.

Note. Shower-stall walls can be made of laminated plastic or enameled hardboard like that discussed on page 86. In the narrow confines of the average stall, however, I recommend against them because of the possibilities of leaks developing at the corners.

PLUMBING FIXTURES—SINKS

Requirements. Not damaged by blows; resist soiling and staining; easy to clean.

Types available. Porcelain enamel on cast iron; stainless steel; porcelain enamel on steel.

Choice. From the best to least good—in the order given above. Stainless steel shows soil, and even though it is not hard to wipe or wash clean, it continues to look smudged. Porcelain enamel is even easier to clean—and looks it when it is. Furthermore, porcelain enamel on cast iron is very resistant to hard blows. On steel, however, the enamel chips readily.

103

PLUMBING FIXTURES—TOILETS

Requirements. Toilets wash down clean and do not clog; flushing mechanism works reliably, does not corrode or get out of alignment; toilet seats do not chip, warp or discolor; hinges do not rust.

Types available. Wall-hung and pedestal type. Wash-down, reverse-trap and siphon-action designs.

Choice. All toilets are made of vitreous china; but the quality of the china improves as the toilet prices rise.

Wash-down toilets are the cheapest and require the most maintenance because they have the least efficient cleaning action. Reverse-trap toilets are medium in cost and better on all scores. Best of all are toilets with siphon action, for although they are expensive, they clean themselves thoroughly. They are also the quietest.

Additional advantage of siphon-action toilets is that some models are made in one piece. This prevents leaks between bowl and tank. However, leaks in two-piece toilets are very rare.

The quality of the materials in the flushing mechanism increases with the cost of the toilet. The best seats are made of high-impact, fade-resistant plastic and have nylon hinges.

In choosing a toilet, you should note one other point: While the great majority are bolted to the floor, a few models are hung on the wall. The latter greatly simplify cleaning of the bathroom because you can swish a mop under them and clean the floor in a second. By contrast, you cannot clean thoroughly under a pedestal toilet without getting down on hands and knees; and even to do a halfway job takes a minute or so.

Both siphon-action and reverse-trap wall-hung toilets are available.

PLUMBING FIXTURES—SHOWER CURTAINS AND SHOWER DOORS FOR TUBS

Requirements. Prevent water from leaking onto the bathroom floor; resist staining; clean easily; do not interfere with cleaning of the tub and walls above it.

Types available. Sliding glass and plastic doors; bifold glass doors; accordion doors of rigid plastic; curtains.

Choice. Sliding doors are an invention of the devil because they interfere with your use of the tub enclosure and make cleaning doubly difficult since you can reach into only one half of the enclosure at a time.

Bifold doors, which open back against the rear wall of the enclosure, and accordion doors, which can be pushed to either end of the enclosure, simplify cleaning. Of the two, the bifold doors are preferable because there are fewer joints which might bind or otherwise get out of whack.

One drawback of all rigid tub-enclosure doors is that they slide in a metal track which needs to be cleaned occasionally.

Whatever the construction of doors, they should be made of translucent rather than transparent material so they will not show water spots. Glass doors should also be made of tempered glass.

Shower curtains are anything but watertight, but their performance can be improved by hanging a decorative curtain on the outside and a waterproof vinyl curtain inside. Liners with magnets in the bottom edge stick tight against the inside wall of the tub. Leaks at the end of the tub can be largely prevented if the end walls are constructed with pockets, or returns, which the liner curtain can be tucked into.

A second disadvantage of shower curtains is that they soil and become mildewed and then require cleaning (which may not be easy). They may also tear.

PLUMBING FIXTURES—TUBS

Requirements. Clean easily; resist chipping.

Types available. Porcelain-enamel-on-steel and porcelain-enamel-on-cast-iron tubs; fiberglass tub enclosures; ceramic-tile tubs built to order. Conventional and sunken tubs. Rectangular and square tubs.

Choice. Porcelain-enamel-on-cast-iron tubs are most resistant to damage; and along with porcelain-enamel-on-steel and fiberglass, they are the easiest to clean. (If the fiberglass tub enclosure is considered only as a tub, it ranks slightly behind

105

porcelain-enamel-on-cast-iron tubs. But as a tub enclosure, it has advantages. See interior walls—bathrooms.)

Conventional tubs resting on the floor joists are much easier to clean than sunken tubs; and rectangular tubs are considered easier to clean than square tubs because you do not have to stretch to reach the back wall.

Note. Many new porcelain-enamel tubs have a very slightly roughened bottom to make them skidproof. Unfortunately, this also makes them a bit harder to clean. But this is a minor drawback to a splendid feature.

PLUMBING SYSTEM—DRAINS

Requirements. Resist clogging, corrosion, breakage.

Types available. Copper, galvanized steel, cast-iron and plastic pipe for inside the house; cast-iron, vitreous enamel, composition and plastic pipe for outside.

Choice. Inside, use copper or plastic. Their smooth surfaces resist clogging better than other materials. Outside, the choice is pretty much a toss-up, with cast iron and plastic getting a slight nod.

Note. Plastic drains are not permitted in many communities.

PLUMBING SYSTEM—WATER LINES

Requirements. Resist corrosion and clogging.

Types available. Copper; galvanized iron; rigid plastic.

Choice. Copper. Galvanized iron is satisfactory in some areas, but not many; besides, if it does need to be repaired, the work is usually harder for the plumber and more expensive for you.

Plastic pipe might well be top choice in the future, but it has not been in use long enough for us to know how durable and trouble-free it is.

PLYWOOD

Used for structural purposes (sheathing, roof deck, subfloors).

Requirements. Provides a strong, rigid nailing surface that will not delaminate. In subfloors under resilient and seamless flooring, the plywood must also provide a smooth surface to support the flooring evenly.

Choice. For walls, roofs and wood floors, use standard interior-grade plywood with a C face. For subfloors under resilient and seamless flooring, use interior-grade plywood underlayment with a C (Plugged) face. In all cases, the thickness of plywood used depends on the spacing of the joists or studs.

RANGES

Requirements. Operate efficiently and without costly service for fifteen to twenty years; fit tight against adjoining counters and cabinets; easy to clean inside and out; have a finish that resists heat, scratching, acids, alkalies, etc.; oven and broiler doors operate easily and close tight.

Types available. Gas and electric ranges of several designs.

Choice. Except on one score, all ranges are about equally easy to maintain. They operate efficiently; need almost no service except for moving parts such as switches and timers; and are finished in tough porcelain enamel or stainless steel.

But when it comes to cleaning, there is a big difference between available models. To make life easier for yourself, choose a range with the following features:

1. It is designed so that there are no open cracks between the sides and the adjoining counters and cabinets. Such crevices are almost impossible to clean when food and liquids spill into them.

2. The entire top of the range, including the burners, is covered with a seamless sheet of heat-resistant, unbreakable glass-ceramic. No other range surface is so easy to keep clean.

3. The control panel is as flat and smooth as possible, and the control knobs, buttons, etc. are spaced far enough apart so you can easily clean around them. (There is no choice between a control panel on the front of a range and one on the backsplash: in the long run, both collect about the same amount of grease, etc. But when the controls are mounted on the range surface, they need much more frequent cleaning.)

4. The control knobs have no grease-catching, hard-to-clean groovings, and can be pulled off so you can wash them at the sink.

5. The oven and broiler are self-cleaning.

REFRIGERATORS AND FREEZERS

Requirements. Operate efficiently and without costly service for fifteen years; resist scarring and deterioration of the finish; easy to clean and clean behind; do not need defrosting; doors close and open properly; shelves are easy to clean and do not warp or break; crispers, liners, ice makers, etc. resist breaking.

Types available. Single-door refrigerators; two-door refrigerators of three designs; chest and upright freezers.

Choice. Defrosting is the biggest chore in running a refrigerator and freezer; therefore the model to choose is one that defrosts itself completely and automatically. If you are buying a single-door refrigerator, choose a model with automatic defrosting. If you are buying a two-door refrigerator, choose a frost-free, or no-frost, model in which both compartments are kept free of frost. (In a two-door model with automatic defrosting, only the fresh-food compartment is kept free of frost.) If you are buying a freezer—either an upright or a chest—choose a frost-free model.

Shelves which are made of thin, stainless-steel wires and which lift out easily not only need less cleaning, but are also easier to clean than other kinds. Solid shelves which cover the meat and vegetable crispers are best made of tempered glass —not plastic.

Refrigerators on casters can be rolled out from the wall so you can get at the dust and dirt behind them more easily.

Note. If you buy a refrigerator or freezer that meets the three tests above, you have gone about as far as you can to reduce upkeep. I must point out, however, that while no-frost and automatic-defrost refrigerators and freezers eliminate a tedious maintenance job, they are more complicated than models you must defrost by hand; consequently, they may give you considerable trouble requiring service from the dealer or manufacturer during the first couple of years. A refrigerator which also has an automatic ice maker may cause even more trouble.

One other point to remember when buying a refrigerator or freezer is that many parts are made of plastic. Cast a critical eye on these. Examine particularly shelf supports and the way in which the fronts of door shelves are attached to the door (which is covered on the inside with plastic).

It's true that you cannot avoid plastic parts in refrigerators and freezers; in fact, more and more are being used. It is also true that many plastic parts will last "forever." But some of those that are subject to stress and handling are likely to disintegrate in short order.

REFUSE-DISPOSAL DEVICES

Requirements. Save steps; do not contribute to kitchen mess and the resultant need for cleaning; get rid of or store trash safe from dogs and raccoons, which may scatter it across the landscape; prevent littering of the grounds when trash is collected; do not require cleaning.

Types available. Metal and rigid-plastic garbage cans; garbage disposers; incinerators; compactors; paper garbage bags; plastic garbage bags.

Choice. The compactor is a new electrical appliance which compresses the equivalent of three or four ordinary garbage canfuls of refuse into a polyethylene-wrapped cube 10 x 16 x 16 inches. The device has not been in use long enough for us to know how useful and reliable it is. But it seems to come closest of all the devices named to meeting requirements. Because it is installed under the counter in the kitchen—usually next to the sink—and because it handles *all* kinds of refuse, there is little mess, little walking to dump trash. You need to go outside only when one of the cubes is completed and ready for pickup. There is no mess outdoors. And because the garbage is compressed into a plastic bag, little cleaning of the compactor is necessary.

Disposers are extremely useful and cut down on kitchen mess, but get rid only of food waste (which accounts for a mere 7 per cent of the total volume of household refuse). So you must still use some kind of outdoor container.

Incinerators burn up everything that is combustible, but not glass, metal, etc., which must be dumped in outdoor containers. The main drawback of incinerators is the fact that they must be vented into a Class-A chimney, which means they are usually installed in the basement or utility room, remote from the kitchen. Consequently, you must carry dripping garbage through the kitchen to dispose of it. You must also clean the ashes out of the incinerator every week or so.

Paper garbage bags are amazingly durable 30-gallon containers which take the place of conventional garbage cans. They can be hung in roll-about racks in the kitchen and carried outside when full; but they are usually hung outside in wall racks. They are a big improvement over metal or rigid-plastic garbage cans because they are thrown onto the garbage truck with the trash they contain—in other words, they never need to be cleaned. And there is no spillage on the ground for the same reason. They do not, of course, save steps or reduce kitchen mess any more than conventional garbage cans do. And they are no more dogproof or raccoonproof. But they are highly recommended by sanitary engineers and are being required by more and more U. S. communities. Used in conjunction with disposers, they are almost as good from every standpoint—including upkeep— as compactors.

Plastic garbage bags when made of 3-mil polyethylene are exactly like paper bags. But the 1.5-mil bags most commonly used serve only as liners for conventional garbage cans. Easily punctured by sharp objects, they occasionally break when taken to the garbage truck. And while they keep garbage cans clear, they do not completely eliminate the need for washing the cans.

Conventional garbage cans are unacceptable.

ROOF DECKS

Used for sunning, entertaining, etc.

Requirements. Watertight; resistant to weathering; resistant to wear, fire, staining; easily repaired.

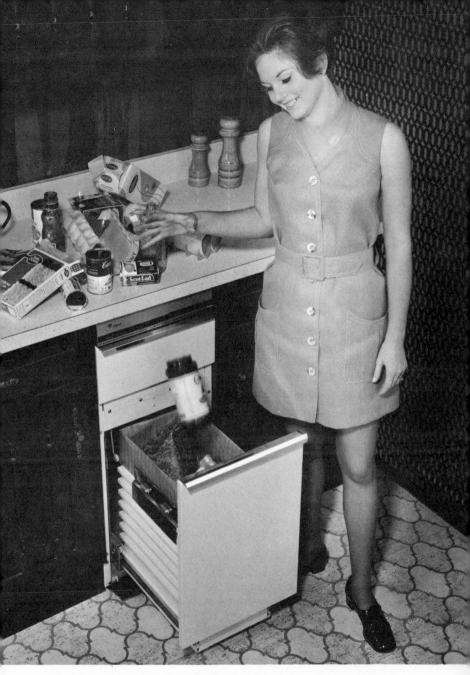

Garbage compactor is a new kitchen appliance which disposes of all kinds of refuse by squeezing it into a small cube wrapped in plastic. (Whirlpool Corp.)

Types available. Canvas; silicone rubber; rubber; seamless flooring made of epoxy and ultraviolet-resistant ceramic granules.

Choice. Silicone rubber or seamless flooring are in first place; rubber in second; canvas in third.

Little is actually known about the durability of the two rubber and seamless decks, because all are new products; but the experience of assorted users indicates that routine upkeep is minimal. Canvas, on the other hand, requires constant attention, and even then does not last awfully long.

ROOFS—FLAT OR ALMOST FLAT

Requirements. Keep out the weather; long-lasting; easy to repair; fire-resistant.

Types available. Copper and terne sheets laid with flat-locked seams; built-up tar and gravel; rubber.

Choice. In the order listed. For explanation, see the entry following.

ROOFS—SLOPING

Requirements. Keep out the weather; long-lasting; easy to repair; fire-resistant.

Types available. Asbestos-cement shingles; asphalt shingles; built-up tar and gravel; asphalt roll roofing; aluminum; clay tile; copper; rubber; slate; terne; wood shingles and shakes; urethane foam.

Choice. Asbestos-cement shingles, clay tile and copper will last indefinitely and never require attention; but they are about the most expensive materials available. In addition, asbestos-cement shingles and clay tiles are difficult to replace if broken by a falling tree limb.

Slate falls in almost exactly the same category; but has a greater tendency to break and is equally hard to repair.

Corrugated aluminum sheets also can be expected to last a lifetime without trouble, provided they are not exposed to salt spray or a corrosive atmosphere. They are anything but pretty, however. Aluminum shingles with a baked-on finish eventually lose their finish—at which point you must

112

Roof of cedar shakes is more handsome than one of ordinary shingles, but presents the same problems and advantages. Stains on the roof under the chimney are unavoidable and cannot be erased. They would occur on all roofs but would be less pronounced on those with less texture because rain would wash them off to a certain extent. (Photo from "America's Great Private Gardens")

either apply a new and less durable finish or allow them to glint in the sun. They give few problems otherwise. Both materials are of medium cost.

Terne is an expensive steel sheet coated with lead-tin alloy. A roof made of it should last indefinitely as long as it is repainted about every ten years with an acrylic paint.

By contrast, galvanized steel sheets are one of the least costly roofing materials, but have a life expectancy of only fifteen to forty years, depending on the climate. They must be kept painted. Some sheets, however, are sold with a tough baked-on finish.

Asphalt roll roofing and asphalt shingles are the least expensive materials. A good grade of either product has a normal life expectancy of twenty years, but this can be extended somewhat by applying an asphalt-aluminum coating. To prevent wind from getting under the roofing and ripping it, you should cement the shingle tabs and lower edges of the rolled strips. If either material is torn or punctured, a repair can be made quickly and inexpensively.

Built-up tar and gravel roofing should not be used on roofs with a pitch of more than 3 inches in 12 inches. A medium-cost roof, it also has a life expectancy of twenty years and is easy to repair when it is damaged.

Wood shingles are costly and require more maintenance than other materials because they may split or curl. In damp, shaded locations they may also become covered with moss. A roof in which the shingles are nailed to spaced furring strips and which is exposed mainly to the sun can be expected to last twenty-five to thirty years. But if the shingles are laid on a solid deck or if the roof is shaded, you will probably have to replace it in about fifteen years. A further disadvantage of wood shingles is that they are combustible, although it is worth noting that fires originating on roofs of *any* kind are extremely rare. (Furthermore, the Koppers Company sells a wood shingle that is resistant to fire.)

Rubber is an expensive liquid roofing material which is applied with a brush or roller. Its great advantage is the fact that it will make a roof of any shape or configuration completely waterproof; and it is easy to maintain and repair. But it is so new that its life expectancy is not known.

Urethane foam can also be used on a roof of any shape. Applied by spraying to a new roof deck or over any sound old roofing, it seals out water, adds rigidity to the roof and is an excellent insulator. The cost is fairly high. Life expectancy has not been determined.

SCREEN CLOTH

Requirements. Does not wear out, stain walls below or require refinishing; stays straight under pressure.

Types available. Aluminum; aluminum with baked-on enamel finish; fiberglass.

Choice. Forget ordinary aluminum: it corrodes. In window screens, use either aluminum with baked-on finish or fiberglass. They meet all requirements. In doors, finished aluminum is preferred because it resists bellying when pushed with hands, knees and elbows or when scratched by dogs.

SCREENS

Requirements. Easy to put up and take down; do not require refinishing; do not warp, shrink or swell; doors are easy to clean; screen cloth raises no problems (see preceding entry).

Types available. Combination screen and storm windows of aluminum; combination screen and storm doors of aluminum or wood; aluminum-framed window screens; wood-framed window screens; tension screens for windows; wood-framed doors; aluminum-framed doors.

Choice. In areas where storm sash is needed, three-track combination screens are outstanding labor savers because you can convert from screen to storm window in a couple of seconds and without any effort: Similarly, combination doors save work—but by no means as much work—because it is much easier to take out the screen inserts and put in glass inserts—and vice versa—than it is to remove an entire screen door and replace it with a storm door.

Of the combination windows and doors, the best and easiest to maintain are made of heavyweight aluminum with

Window screens made with narrow aluminum frames are very light-weight and easy to put up and take down, and they take up much less space in storage than wood-framed screens. They are also very unobtrusive when installed in windows. (Unlike the screens, which require little maintenance, the louvered shutters of wood are a headache.)

baked-enamel finish. The doors are 1¼ inches thick, and are prehung in aluminum casings to prevent air and water leakage.

If you don't need storm sash, use screens with narrow aluminum frames finished in baked enamel in all windows you can reach from the ground. In higher windows, use tension screens. These actually are a little more troublesome to put up and take down than framed screens, but you can do the job from inside. In addition, the screens are lighter; and since they roll up like a window shade, they are more maneuverable. But they are not recommended for first-floor windows because they are more perishable.

An additional argument that is made in favor of tension screens is that you can just push them out of your way when washing windows on the outside. But they are, in fact, no easier to handle than framed screens.

If you do not need a storm door, use a simple screen door with a rigid aluminum frame with baked-enamel finish.

In short, don't bother with wood-framed door or window screens. But note that this does not mean that all aluminum-framed screens are good, because they are not. Only the more expensive, quality products are easy to maintain.

SHELVES, OPEN

Used for books, records, decorative objects, etc.

Requirements. Easy to clean; resist scarring and staining; need no refinishing; do not sag or warp.

Types available. Actually, you can use just about any strong, flat, reasonably thin material that comes to hand; but for practical purposes, shelves are usually made of wood, plate glass or laminated plastic bonded to wood or flakeboard.

Choice. Laminated-plastic shelves—preferably those with a pattern rather than a solid color.

Glass is a good second choice, although dust and finger-marks show up clearly and cleaning must be more frequent.

If shelves are made of wood, best results are obtained by covering them with Type B vinyl wallcovering. Painted shelves become stained and scarred when used for active book

117

and record storage; and shelves with a clear finish also show wear.

Note. Any shelf will sag if not properly supported.

SHUTTERS

Requirements. Slow to soil; easy to clean; do not require painting; resist cracking and breaking.

Types available. Wood, prefinished aluminum or vinyl made in louvered, paneled or vertical-board designs.

Choice. Vinyl and aluminum are superior to wood on all scores. But all shutters are made with louvers, and these collect much more dirt and are harder to clean than other designs. Even so, vinyl is the winner; aluminum, the runner-up.

Note. If you use wood shutters, make sure they have been treated with wood preservative.

SOFFITS

Used under roof overhangs.

Requirements. Do not require painting.

Types available. Wood and plywood painted at the site; prefinished plywood and hardboard; factory-finished aluminum; vinyl.

Choice. Vinyl, because it is colored clear through; there is no coating to peel off.

STORM SASH

Used in windows and doors in colder climates.

Requirements. Easy to put up and take down; do not require refinishing; do not warp, shrink or swell; will not fly off in heavy winds; clean easily; permit easy cleaning of permanent windows.

Types available. Combination screen and storm windows of aluminum; combination screen and storm doors of aluminum or wood; aluminum-framed windows; wood-framed windows; wood-framed doors.

Choice. Combinations made of quality aluminum with baked-enamel finish. Windows should have three tracks so that the two glass inserts and the screen insert can be slid up and down and taken in and out independently of one another. Doors should be 1¼ inches thick and prehung in aluminum casings to prevent air and water leakage.

VENTILATING FANS

Requirements. Remove from the kitchen the maximum of water vapor, grease smoke and odors; long-lasting; easy to clean.

Types available. Ducted and non-ducted hood fans; ducted wall and ceiling fans.

Choice. See page 40. Whichever type of fan is installed be sure it has the largest CFM capacity available; otherwise it will do only a partial job of getting rid of water vapor and grease.

WASHERS AND DRYERS

Requirements. Operate efficiently for at least ten to twelve years respectively with a minimum of servicing; easy to clean.

Types available. Automatic, wringer and spinner washers; electric and gas dryers; combination washer-dryers.

Choice. Low cost and simplicity of operation are here synonymous with ease of maintenance.

Wringer washers, followed by spinner washers require less servicing than automatics, because they are much less complicated machines. For the same reason, automatic washers and automatic dryers individually require less servicing than combination washer-dryers. (The two together, however, may require more servicing than a combination by itself.)

Similarly, low-cost automatic washers and low-cost dryers with the minimum number of controls and features require less servicing than higher-cost machines with more controls and features.

WATER HEATERS

Requirements. Supply ample hot water at no less than 140 degrees and preferably at 160 degrees with a minimum of servicing for at least ten years; tanks do not corrode and leak, and resist scaling.

Types available. Gas, electric and oil-fired storage heaters with galvanized steel, glass-lined, copper or copper-on-steel tanks; tankless take-off heaters; indirect storage heaters.

Choice. Tankless take-off heaters and indirect storage heaters are essentially the same thing: a coil of copper tube attached to an automatic hot-water or steam boiler. Water circulating through the tube is heated by the hot water in the boiler. In a tankless heater, the water is then piped directly to the faucets. In an indirect storage heater, it is piped into a small storage tank from which it then goes on to the faucets.

Because these heaters have no moving parts, they require less service than storage heaters—provided your water does not contain elements that build up a scale deposit in the copper coil. If your water contains these undesirable elements, you will probably have to call in a serviceman every year or so to purge the coil with acid.

Among the storage heaters, the oil-fired units are the only ones which must be serviced annually to clean and adjust the burner. Both oil and gas heaters have flues which may occasionally rust out. On electric water heaters the heating elements sometimes wear out. But there is actually little difference in the amount of maintenance the three heaters require—*if* you buy them intelligently.

By "intelligently," I mean three things:

1. Make sure you buy a storage water heater that is properly sized for your needs. (All water-heater dealers and plumbers have tables which give proper sizes.) If your heater is undersized, it must work harder to produce the hot water you want, and this causes it to break down faster.

2. Select a tank material which will resist the action of your water. If your water is very corrosive, you should install a solid-copper or copper-on-steel tank. They are quite expensive but will last a long time. Glass-lined tanks cost less but generally do well in moderately corrosive waters. Galvanized tanks are least resistant to corrosion, although they

may do well in hard-water areas because they build up a scale deposit which protects them.

3. Buy a top-quality heater that is covered by a long-term guarantee. The guarantee should provide that if the heater fails while in warranty, the manufacturer will make some provision to provide you with hot water until repairs or replacements are made.

WATER PUMPS

Used to supply water to the house from a well.

Requirements. Operate efficiently for many years with minimum servicing; resist corrosion.

Types available. Jet and submersible pumps.

Choice. A submersible pump, but only if your well is fairly deep. In a shallow well, a jet pump is usually more desirable, for although it needs somewhat more servicing, it has a low initial cost.

WATER TANKS

Used in home water systems for storing well water and providing it under pressure.

Requirements. Do not corrode; withstand the pressure of the air cushion; do not cause a condensation problem in the summer.

Types available. Galvanized tanks; glass-lined galvanized tanks; glass-lined and insulated galvanized tanks.

Choice. Don't worry about any water tank's ability to withstand the air pressure under which the water system operates. Unless the pressure is most unusually high, all will be safe.

For long, maintenance-free life, the glass-lined tank is the more reliable because it resists corrosion; however, you should note that in a cold-water tank, corrosion is much less of a problem than in a water-heater tank.

The glass-lined, insulated tank is the most expensive but is recommended if the tank is installed in a utility room, kitchen or some other place where the condensation forming on the tank can flood or stain the floor. However, fiberglass jackets are available for uninsulated tanks.

WINDOWS

Requirements. Operate easily; close tight; easy to wash; do not need refinishing.

Types available. Double-hung, sliding, casement, awning, hopper and jalousie windows made of wood, vinyl-clad wood, aluminum or steel.

Choice. In a nutshell, the windows which require the least maintenance over the years are double-hung and sliding units with aluminum frames and removable or tilting sash for easy washing. This, however, is an extreme simplification of the situation, and you should not make a selection without considering the maintenance pros and cons of each window type and construction.

Double-hung windows don't warp or sag because they are held in tracks. They operate easily, without requiring adjustment. But wood sash, if not properly seasoned and treated with a preservative containing a water repellent, may stick. They may also stick if painted sloppily. They are reasonably easy to wash from inside the house if the sash are removable or designed so they can be tilted out from the casing. But they admit rain, which causes a secondary maintenance problem, when open.

Sliding windows have the same maintenance advantages and disadvantages as double-hungs.

Casements may sag and warp, and become difficult to close tight. The hinges and the lever or crank used to adjust the sash need to be lubricated periodically. When open wide, the windows admit rain; and the sash themselves require more maintenance because they become wet outside and in. They are easy enough to wash on both sides from inside the house as long as they are hinged so that you can reach between the sash and the frame. Since screens are installed inside the window, they are very easy to put up and take down, and are protected from the weather.

Awning windows are not likely to warp or sag, although they sometimes do. The adjusting mechanism must be lubricated periodically to keep it operating easily. The sash collect more dirt than the three previous windows, but they

122

can be washed easily from inside the house as long as you can reach your arm between the upper sash and frame. They keep out rain. Screens are installed inside.

Hopper windows, opening inward and downward, are rarely used in homes except in clerestories and basements. They usually have only a single sash which operates easily (although I have seen some exceptions). They rarely warp or sag; are easy to wash from inside the house. They admit rain only if the sash is pivoted rather than hinged.

Jalousies should be used only in milder climates since they admit some air. They can, however, be combined with inside storm windows. The operating mechanism is more complicated than that on other types of window and consequently requires more maintenance. While the panes (louvers) can be washed from inside the house, the process is very slow and tedious. The windows admit a great deal of dust, even when closed, when the wind is blowing hard. On the other hand, rain cannot enter the house unless the panes are slanted upward. If panes are broken, they are readily replaced without glazing compound.

Wood-framed windows require more maintenance than other constructions although wood is the only material which you can be sure of at the seashore. Stock windows are usually made with wood that is treated at the factory with a preservative and water repellent, so you do not need to worry about decay. These windows also have good dimensional stability, though they may swell and stick in very hot weather. But they need to be refinished frequently.

Steel windows also need to be painted frequently to keep them looking neat and to prevent rusting. The work is complicated by the fact that the painting surfaces adjacent to the glass on the inside are extremely narrow. On the other hand, once you have painted a steel window there is almost nothing you must do to it.

Aluminum windows require little maintenance, except at the seashore where you must use rugged, anodized alloys if you don't want severe pitting and corrosion. If you dislike the white oxide that forms on aluminum, you should also occasionally apply lacquer to the frames. One other advantage of aluminum windows: reglazing is made simply with a snap-in vinyl glazing bead.

Vinyl-clad wood window frames are a fairly new development; but, unfortunately, they are found only on casement, awning and fixed windows. The sash are made of treated wood completely covered with off-white rigid vinyl. Exterior exposed surfaces of the casings are also covered with off-white vinyl. The result: No painting is required except on the inside trim. Reglazing is simplified with a snap-in vinyl glazing bead.

WINDOWS—SILLS

Requirements. Clean with a swish of a rag; resist wear; do not need refinishing.

Types available. Wood, finished in the home with paint, clear finish, vinyl wallcoverings, laminated plastic, ceramic tile, etc.; prefabricated sills of marble and fiberglass.

Choice. Either of the prefabricated sills or a sill covered with laminated plastic.

cabinets or in wood cabinets lined with aluminum sheets. Store bedding, mattresses and other linens in big chests, drawers or benches which are also lined with aluminum. Make sure that openings around all pipes entering the house are sealed. Cover chimney tops with wire mesh to keep out squirrels as well as birds.

Although it is almost impossible to deny mice and rats admission to a house, you can do a pretty good job of keeping them out of the kitchen and other rooms and closets if you make a thorough search for holes and large cracks. Check particularly around water pipes, drains, heating pipes and electric cables under or behind kitchen and laundry appliances. Check also for breaks in plaster walls in closets and for wide cracks between floors and baseboards. Be sure the inside door to the basement fits tight to the floor.

One popular point of entry for mice is through holes in the wall and floor areas concealed by kitchen base cabinets and bathroom vanity cabinets. These holes, alas, are very hard to find and to close once the cabinets are installed. But if you build or remodel, make a point of inspecting the kitchen and bathroom walls and floors *before* the cabinets go in. Holes that are found can be sealed with patches of aluminum flashing securely nailed on all edges. If patches are difficult to fit, stuff the holes tightly with coarse steel wool.

APPLIANCES

Don't abuse your appliances. Manufacturers who keep records of their service calls have discovered that a lot of these are unnecessary and a lot that are necessary stem from careless handling of the appliances. Here's what you should and should not do to keep your equipment in good operating condition:

All appliances. Read the instruction book for each new appliance carefully, and then file it away for ready reference. Even though the appliance may be only a new model of a piece of equipment you have used for years, it undoubtedly has some unfamiliar features which require special attention. As one home economist told me some years ago: "Every woman knows how to use an iron, but this doesn't necessarily mean she knows how to use a steam iron. Yet she starts using it without opening the instruction book. And then eventually she does something that actually damages the iron or simply makes her think the iron isn't operating properly and needs to be taken to a service station."

Make sure the appliance is properly installed. If it isn't, it may not function efficiently and there may even be damage to the appliance. For example, if you build a television set into a tight-fitting, unventilated cabinet, the heat given off by the tubes cannot escape and the tubes will wear out rapidly. Similarly, a refrigerating mechanism deteriorates faster than it should if the heat given off is not allowed to escape into the kitchen.

Make sure your wiring system has enough circuits and big enough wires to deliver the power that your electric appliances require. If the wiring does not deliver adequate power, the appliances will not be harmed (though they will not function properly), but you will probably spend a lot of time running down to the basement to replace fuses or reset circuit breakers—an altogether needless maintenance chore. If you attempt to correct this situation—as many people have—by putting in larger fuses than the wiring is designed for, the wiring in the walls will overheat and perhaps start a fire, appliance motors may burn out—any number of serious problems may arise.

If possible, don't allow electric motors on appliances and also on water pumps, furnaces, swimming-pool filters, etc. to become immersed in water. It knocks them out, but does not damage them seriously unless you try to restart them while they are wet. In that case, they will burn out and require major repairs. The proper procedure to follow if a motor is flooded is to unplug it at once and ask a motor-repair shop to bake it out.

If your voltage drops sharply for any period of time, causing your lights to become very dim and electric clocks to stop, turn off or unplug all large motor-driven appliances and other large motors. Do not turn them on again until after the voltage returns to normal. If you fail to do this, the motor may be damaged by the sudden surge of power that hits them when the voltage drop is corrected.

Although modern appliances are often permanently lubricated by the manufacturer and do not require oiling, read the instruction book and make certain this is true of your appliances. Then apply oil if and as called for.

Blenders. To keep from damaging the cutting blades on the impeller, do not put ice cubes into the container by themselves. If the cubes are being used to chill a drink, add them one at a time to the mixture in the container.

Dishwashers. Don't place cutlery with very slim handles or forks with long, widely spaced tines in the silver basket, thin end down. They may fall part way through the basket and jam, dent or break the revolving spray arm underneath.

Rinse large, hard food particles off plates before washing them. They may clog the drain pump, especially in older dishwashers.

While chlorine bleach is recommended for use in dishwashers to remove coffee and tea stains from utensils and cups, you should not use more than a teaspoonful at a time and you should not use it more than once a month; otherwise some of the dishwasher parts may be harmed.

Vinegar may also damage dishwasher parts if used more than twice a month to get rid of mineral deposits and spots caused by very hard water.

Disposers. Always use non-caustic drain cleaners in a disposer if the drain below it becomes clogged (which rarely happens, because the food particles ground up in the disposer usually keep the drain scoured clean). Caustic cleaners are likely to cause corrosion of disposer parts.

To keep a disposer from jamming, never put into it wastes which the manufacturer advises against. These vary between makes but may include bones, fruit pits, fibrous material such as cornhusks and asparagus stalks, and paper goods.

Be careful not to drop cutlery into the grinding chamber. It will be ruined and the grinding mechanism may be damaged, too.

Dryers. Never put plastic baby pants and similar materials in a dryer. They may go up in smoke, taking dryer and house with them. Articles which have been soaked in cleaning fluid are equally volatile until they have been washed thoroughly. The same is true of rubber articles and of cleaning cloths and mops impregnated with chemicals and wax.

There is also a fire-hazard if you operate your dryer when the lint trap is not in place and when you operate it with the lint trap too full. (It should be cleaned before each load.)

Electric frying pans and saucepans. Don't immerse the electrical control—whether it is removable or a permanent part of the pan—in water.

Freezers. See refrigerators.

Irons. The newest steam irons can be filled with ordinary tap water. But unless your iron is guaranteed to resist clogging, your best bet—to prolong its usefulness—is to fill it with distilled water. This is especially important if your tap water is hard.

To prevent corrosion of the soleplate, empty the steam iron after it is used, or store it on its heel.

Don't scratch the soleplate of any iron by ironing over zippers or metal snaps.

Despite the claims of spray-starch manufacturers, I have yet to find one of these products which does not stain the soleplate of an iron. Unless you enjoy removing the stains, use an old-fashioned starch.

Mixers. To keep the beaters from becoming badly bent and perhaps ruined, don't use a metal knife, fork or spoon while running it. Use a rubber spatula only.

Ranges. When cleaning or removing the drip pans under electric-range units, raise the units carefully to avoid breaking the electric leads.

Don't heat a very large, flat pot or pan on a small burner at high heat for a long time: the heat may craze the porcelain-enamel surface surrounding the burner and shorten the life of an electric element. You can damage an electric-oven floor in the same way if you place a large sheet of aluminum foil just above the heating element so that the element is almost sealed off from the rest of the oven.

Rotate the use of electric surface units as much as possible. If you use one almost exclusively, it is likely to wear out fairly soon. The switch controlling it will also wear out. On the other hand, if all units are given more or less normal use, they should last about as long as you want to keep the range.

Refrigerators. Unless you enjoy buying new ice trays, don't put undue pressure on the divider handles if the ice is frozen as hard as a rock. Let the tray thaw a few minutes.

Don't use the built-in door shelves as handles to pull the door shut. The shelves and door liner are made of plastic which may crack.

Don't use cleaning fluids, wax cleaners or polishes to clean the refrigerator liner and other plastic refrigerator parts. Use soda or mild detergent only.

On manual-defrost models, it's quite permissible—in fact a good idea—to hasten thawing of the ice by putting ice trays filled with warm water in the ice-cube compartment. But never use an electric defroster, because the high heat may do untold damage to plastic surfaces, insulation on wires, controls, etc.

Vacuum cleaners. Pick up pins, tacks and other metal objects from the floor before they are sucked into the vacuum cleaner and jam it.

Washers. Turn off water inlets after using the washer. If you don't, the water pressure may burst the hoses or cause leaks at the connections. The resulting flood may damage the laundry floor and ceilings and walls below.

BASEMENTS

Basements which flood in heavy rains because they were not built in the way described on page 16 should be protected with a sump pump which automatically removes the water when it reaches a predetermined depth in the sump.

BOILERS

Drain hot-water boilers infrequently, and then only enough to draw off sediment. The reason for this is that when water is heated repeatedly in a heating system, it loses its oxygen and becomes non-corrosive. You should therefore avoid adding fresh water, which is full of oxygen, except when it is absolutely necessary. (Water must, however, be added periodically to steam boilers to replace that which is vented through the radiators.)

CARPETS

Stop dirt at the front door with some kind of door mat. If the members of your family have a way of missing the mat right outside the door, cover the entire doorstep or ten feet of the front walk with rough-textured indoor-outdoor carpet. An alternative is to place inside the door a nylon carpet-top like those used in public buildings. These are exceptionally absorbent mats which sponge up moisture to a much greater degree than ordinary door mats.

Use heavy glass coasters under legs of large chairs, tables, etc. to keep them from making deep, often permanent dents in carpets and resilient flooring materials. Use 2¼-inch-wide coasters under beds. Even wood floors can be dented badly by the polished, rounded metal domes which are often tapped into the bottoms of chair legs to make them slide more easily. A perfectly flat chair-leg bottom does less damage.

CEILINGS

Ice dams which form in gutters and also along the edges of roofs without gutters force the melted water running off the roof to back up under the shingles and then drip down through ceilings and walls below. In a new house, this can usually be prevented by installing under the shingles an eaves flashing strip of roll roofing which extends from the drip edge up the roof to a point at least twelve inches inside the inside-wall line. In old houses, the best solution is to lay electric heating cable along the eaves. This should be arranged in a zigzag pattern extending from just beyond the drip edge up the roof for one or two feet. If there is a gutter, a straight run of cable should be laid in the trough from one end to the other; and it should also be led down through the downspout. When the electricity is turned on, the cable cuts channels through the ice dam, allowing the water to run off to the ground.

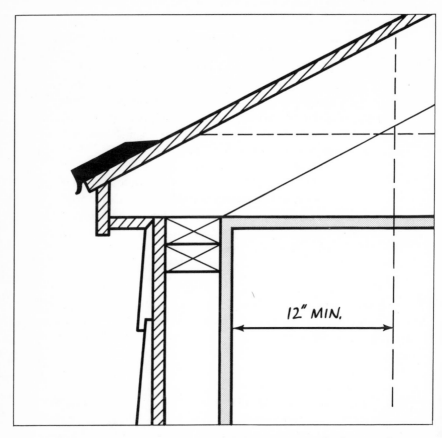

12″ MIN.

In order to prevent ice dams which force water to back up under shingles and cause leaks, an eaves flashing strip of smooth or mineral-surfaced roll roofing should be applied under the shingles and over the drip edge. It should overhang the drip edge and extend back to a point at least 12″ inside the inside-wall line.

CLOSETS

Stop mildew in closets by installing in them one or more incandescent bulbs which are burned constantly during warm, humid weather. One 75-watt bulb is about adequate for a closet with up to six square feet of floor space. Add 25 watts for each additional two square feet or fraction thereof.

COOKING AND TABLE WARE

Keep some things out of the dishwasher: Old china and hand-pointed glassware, because the design may be washed off. Plastic articles which are likely to be melted by the high heat in the drying cycle. Cast-iron utensils, because the detergent removes the grease film which keeps the metal from rusting. Hollow-handled silver knives, because the cement in the handles may be eroded. Woodenware, because the wood is bleached and roughened by the hot detergent solution.

COUNTERS

Give up using cast-iron cooking utensils. Because of their weight, they chip porcelain range and sink surfaces rather readily if accidentally banged against them. And because they hold heat much better than lighter metals, they will burn laminated plastic counters if accidentally set down on them for a few seconds.

DRAPERIES

To protect draperies at windows which are normally left open and through which rain may splash, install slanting glass ventilators above the sills. (Before the days of air conditioning, these were most often used at office windows to let in air and keep out rain and soot.)

DRAWERS

To keep drawers from sticking in damp weather, allow them to dry out to the point where they move easily. Then cover all surfaces with varnish to seal out moisture. You must also varnish the chest on all surfaces that come in contact with the drawers.

Drawers that stick are themselves a nuisance to fix. But another good reason for keeping them loose is to make it unnecessary to put both hands on the front of the drawers in order to close them. Hand oils damage wood finishes in short order.

ELECTRIC CORDS

When unplugging a lamp or appliance, grasp the plug firmly between two fingers and pull it out straight. Never yank the plug out by its cord.

FABRICS

In an existing house, there are three simple ways to keep the sun streaming through windows from fading fabrics and bleaching wood furniture and floors: (1) Hang awnings. (2) Tint the glass. This is done either by flowing or spraying a liquid plastic over the glass or by applying a transparent-plastic film to it. (3) Hang window shades made of a transparent plastic similar to one of the films applied directly to the glass. The obvious advantages that all these measures have over shutters, Venetian blinds and draperies are that they allow you to see out and they also let daylight in. For other solutions which are particularly applicable to new homes, see page 23.

FLOORS

Examine everybody's shoes now and then to make sure that nails are not coming through the heels. More damage is done to floors by shoes in need of repair than by any other single thing.

Insulate cold-water pipes and water tanks to keep them from sweating in warm weather. For one thing, the metal of which they are made may in time start to corrode. But a worse problem is the drip, which may stain the floor on which it falls and puts unwanted water vapor into the air. The best covering for pipes is a spiral-wound ribbon of fiberglass insulation. Fiberglass jackets are available for water tanks.

Transparent plastic film applied to windows cuts the sun's rays and helps to reduce fading of fabrics and flooring materials inside. The film is invisible and permanent and can be cleaned with non-abrasive cloth. (Minnesota Mining & Manufacturing Co.)

To prevent sweating of toilet tanks, line them with plastic insulating sheets made for the purpose. Encasing the tanks in covers made of fabrics to match toilet-seat covers and bath mats also helps a little.

GARAGE FLOORS

Keep your garage floor clean by placing grease pans under the engines of your cars. If you don't want to bother cleaning the pans, line them with aluminum foil or a layer of sand—both of which can be discarded when dirty.

INTERIOR WALLS

To keep doors from banging holes in walls when they are swung open, screw doorstops to the wall or door or attach a hinge-pin stop to one of the door hinges. If for some reason you can't install a doorstop, cushion the doorknob with a rubber or fabric cover made for the purpose. The covers also protect the finish of the knob (but get dirty and wear themselves out).

To prevent water from dripping down behind tubs into the adjacent walls, seal the cracks around the tub rims with crescent-shaped, ceramic edging tiles. They are more permanent, easier to clean and longer lasting than calking compound alone.

IRON AND STEEL ARTICLES

Rustproof ornamental ironwork, iron railings, steel furniture, children's gym equipment, steel window sash and other steel and iron articles used outside the home. If the metal is already rusted, clean it completely with a chisel, file, wire brush, steel wool and liquid or jellied rust remover. Make sure it is dry. Then apply a rust-inhibiting primer—preferably one made with red lead—and paint with trim and shutter enamel.

To keep moisture out of metal joints that are difficult to scrape and seal with paint, fill them with a small bead of polysulfide rubber calking compound. Silicone calking may also be used if it is the kind that can be painted over.

Crescent-shaped tiles are installed in mastic around rim of tub to keep water from dripping down into the walls.

MATTRESSES

Don't sit on the edge of your bed. It breaks down the springs in innerspring mattresses.

MEDICINE CABINETS

Paste vinyl wallcovering to the enameled shelves in medicine cabinets and closets. You can wipe up spilled medicines with a damp cloth; repainting of the shelves is never necessary.

OUTDOOR FAUCETS

Outdoor faucets and water lines which cannot be turned off in winter should be protected from freezing with electric heating cable wrapped in a spiral around them.

OUTDOOR FURNITURE

Keep moisture off terrace furniture which is not made to withstand the onslaught of the elements (that includes most of the furniture built). Either move the furniture under cover when rain threatens or toss lightweight plastic tarpaulins or old shower curtains over them. In windy locations, it's a good idea to tie lead weights to the corners of the tarpaulins.

PAVING

Treat concrete, brick and stone paving with a masonry sealing oil which helps to prevent staining of the surface.

SCREEN DOORS

To keep the screen cloth from being pushed out of shape, install a push bar or grille at hand height inside the door.

SCREWS

When setting or removing screws in latches, coat hooks, etc., use a screwdriver that will not mutilate the slots in the screwheads, thus either wrecking the screws or making them much harder to use again. The screwdriver should have square, not rounded, corners. It should be sharp enough to slip into the slot. And it should be no wider than the slot.

SEASHORE HOMES

Seashore houses that are inundated by high tides and during hurricanes are not unusual in some areas; and while it is impossible to protect them against all damage, they can be kept in operating order, even after flooding, by raising the heating plant and water heater above the level of the highest tide. A water pump in the house should also be raised, or replaced with a submersible pump. All electric outlets, switches, boxes, etc. should be raised, and wires in BX cable or rigid conduit should be replaced with waterproof plastic-sheathed cable, preferably of the type used in underground installations.

The same precautions should be taken in houses subject to flooding by rivers and streams.

SILVERWARE

Because salt corrodes silver rapidly, you should never leave it in silver saltshakers or dishes overnight. This rule also applies to salt dishes that are lined with glass bowls and to shakers made of glass or ceramic with silver tops. After pouring salt out, wash shakers and dishes thoroughly. Wash saltspoons, too.

SWITCH PLATES

Keep electric switch plates from getting grimy by installing perfectly smooth plastic, chromium or solid-brass plates. To protect wall surfaces around switches, install large, transparent-plastic covers over the switch plates.

TABLES

Give tabletops three-way protection—(1) against water spotting, by using thermal glasses made of plastic; (2) against cigarette burns, by using large, deep ashtrays with narrow rims and without cigarette holders (this helps to make people put their cigarettes in the trays—not poised precariously on the rims); (3) against dripping candle wax by using *bobêches* at the base of the candles above the candleholders.

139

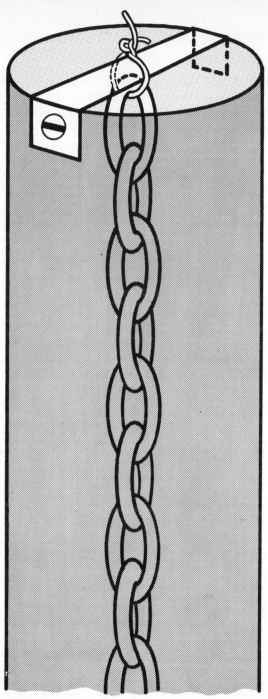

A cable or chain hung inside a television mast helps to keep it from swaying violently in a storm.

UPHOLSTERED FURNITURE

Keep the arms of upholstered chairs and sofas from soiling by covering them with fitted, removable covers made of the same upholstery material. These do not spoil the appearance of the furniture when in use; and they can be taken off and washed or dry-cleaned in a day or two when dirty.

Slipcovers, of course, do the same job, but are more expensive and more troublesome to wash when dirty.

If you believe in miracles, you can treat upholstery with a fluorochemical spray which is supposed to make fabric resistant to watery and oily stains. But I fear you will be disappointed. My own experience has shown these sprays to be almost worthless; and two major organizations that do a great deal of fabric testing agree.

TELEVISION ANTENNAS

To keep tall antenna masts from being buffeted and bent by wind, suspend a steel cable or chain about eighteen to twenty-four inches long inside the top of the mast. The diameter of the cable or chain should be one-third to one-sixth the inside diameter of the mast. When the wind blows, the cable bangs against the sides of the mast and materially dampens the vibrations, thus helping to keep it upright.

(Note that this idea protects antenna masts only against intermittent winds and winds coming from different directions. It is not effective if the wind blows hard and steadily from one direction.)

WALLPAPER

Apply a transparent protective coating available from paint stores to non-washable and semi-washable wallpaper, which is exposed to fingermarking and other soiling.

WATER HEATERS

If you have a water softener, do not heat the water above 140 degrees in an indirect tankless heater with copper coils; otherwise the coils may corrode rapidly.

WINDOWS

Learn to mop kitchen, laundry and bathroom floors with a barely damp mop. When you slosh water on a floor, you fill the air with water vapor which condenses on windows and soon ruins the finish on mullions and sills. The water also seeps down through the seams in resilient floors, loosens the adhesive and eventually causes the floor to crack and curl.

Don't take steam baths and long, hot showers—another major cause of water vapor.

Cook with electricity rather than gas. Tests at Purdue University have shown that 47.5 per cent of the moisture liberated in cooking a week's meals comes from the combustion of gas.

5

Maintenance Methods and Procedures

If I were to put down in this chapter all the ways that Americans go about maintaining the various parts and pieces of their homes, the chapter would turn into a book all by itself; and you would be so hopelessly confused that you would sell your home and move into a hotel.

It really is amazing how many different ways ingenious minds—plus a few confused minds—can dream up to do the same thing—and with often disappointing results.

Just last spring we hired a young man to wash the windows in our house. It happens that we had been badly spoiled by the man we had employed at our previous home. Like all professional window washers, he used nothing more than water and vinegar, a sponge and a collection of squeegees; and in about six hours he could dispose of thirty-four windows plus several doors plus storm sash all the way around for the ridiculous price of sixty dollars. We didn't expect that this new young man would be as speedy; but we did rather hope —since we now lived in a small town in a much less prosperous part of Connecticut—that he would be less—well, no more—expensive.

We should have known better.

Yes, the young man did make a business of washing windows in order to put himself through college. But he was no professional. He was, instead, a reader of advertisements. Or maybe he watched television too much. Anyway, he turned up with an aerosol can of one of the many "miracle" window-washing compounds with which manufacturers are forever gulling millions of unsuspecting housewives. And in the course of two days, for a price of forty-five dollars, he succeeded in cleaning thirty-two windows plus storm sash.

All of which goes to show that there are good ways to maintain a house, and there are also lots of bad ways.

This chapter deals with the good ways. I regret to say that they are not in every case the pluperfect-best ways used by professional maintenance men. This is because professionals (1) often use cleaning compounds, etc. that homeowners cannot buy; (2) they can afford to invest in the special equipment needed to do the best job; and (3) they have the physical strength to use such equipment, much of which is very heavy. But as far as possible, this chapter will give you the simplest and most effective ways to maintain everything from acoustical tile to window shades.

Two other points:

In Chapter 1, I said that the job of maintaining a home includes making the repairs needed to set things right once trouble occurs. This chapter, however, deals only with the *simple* measures needed to keep things going and in good condition. Major repairwork is covered in my book, *How to Fix Almost Everything*.

Second point: The timing given for cleaning and refinishing things is rather arbitrary, though I hope illustrative and not far from the truth. If you live in a remarkably clean village or do no frying, you may be able to go two or three times as long as I have indicated before dusting, cleaning, washing, etc. On the other hand, if you live in New York City, you may have to dust, clean, wash, etc. much more often than indicated.

ACOUSTICAL TILE

To clean: Wash with a not-too-wet sponge dipped in a mild detergent solution; then rinse. If the joints between tiles are tight and not too deep, try washing them from the floor with a sponge-type floor mop with a long handle. This will save work. But if the tile joints are open and deep or if the ceiling is very dirty, you will probably have to get up on a ladder and use a hand sponge.

If you know the tiles are not washable (many are not) or if you find them hard to wash, the only way to clean a ceiling is to vacuum it and then repaint. Note, however, that any grease on the tiles must be removed with detergent before paint is applied.

To remove stains caused by a leak above the ceiling. Try washing. If this is not successful, apply paint: It will not affect the tile's acoustical qualities seriously.

AIR CONDITIONER, CENTRAL

Routine maintenance. Inspect filters every three months and clean or replace them as necessary. Lubricate conditioner at all designated oiling points once a year.

Note. If you have a service contract, the service firm should automatically give you twice-a-year inspection—in the spring and fall.

AIR CONDITIONER, ROOM

Routine maintenance. Clean filters once a month during the cooling season. If you live in the city or an industrial area, the dirt, dust, chemicals, etc. in the air often build up heavily on the condenser, causing a reduction in cooling efficiency and an early burning-out of the cooling mechanism. To prevent this, you should have the air conditioner steam-cleaned every two or three years in fairly clean cities; every year in New York.

Oil fan motor annually. To maintain a conditioner's efficiency and prolong its life when it is installed on the sunny side of the house, screen it from the sun with an awning. To prevent cycling (compressor turning on and off at short intervals), move thermostat up two notches.

ALUMINUM

To clean. Light soil can be washed off with a detergent solution. For heavy soil, scrub with a Naval-jelly rust remover and rinse well. For stubborn stains on non-anodized aluminum, scrub with fine steel wool and Naval jelly; then rinse.

To protect aluminum that is beginning to pit and corrode. Clean thoroughly as above. Remove lingering dirt and oxides with fine steel wool. Prime metal with zinc chromate, and then apply one or two coats of exterior oil paint. If a natural aluminum finish is desired, omit the primer and apply a clear, non-yellowing acrylic or cellulose butyrate lacquer directly to the metal.

To refinish painted aluminum. Clean thoroughly and remove all loose finish. Then prime bare spots with zinc chromate. Repaint the entire surface with exterior oil paint.

AWNINGS, CANVAS

Routine maintenance. Dust thoroughly before hanging awnings in the spring. If they are dirty or stained, scrub with a brush and laundry detergent. (This is easier to do—if you can reach them—after they are hung.) Resew bindings as necessary. Patch small holes or rips by gluing a canvas patch to the underside with white glue made for use on fabrics.

To store. Make sure awnings are completely dry. Fold or roll loosely; but if awnings are on frames, let the fabric hang straight. In other words, don't fold canvas or crumple it any more than necessary. Store in a completely dry place, such as the attic.

BASEMENT AREAWAYS

Routine maintenance. If properly built (see page 17), areaways should cause you little concern. But it's a good idea in the fall to make sure they are not choked with leaves and trash which might cause water to flood through the basement windows. Clean the strainers on the pipes draining into the footing drains. Make sure that the walls of the areaways are in firm contact with the foundation walls.

146

BASEMENT BULKHEADS

Routine maintenance. In the fall, check the calking around the bottom and back edges. Readjust doors as necessary so they close tight. Scrape off loose paint; allow exposed metal or wood to dry; then prime and repaint.

BASEMENT WALLS AND FLOORS

To stop leaks that are developing. If walls are oozing, clean them thoroughly with a stiff bristle brush. Use a wire brush to remove loose paint or other finish. Then scrub two or more coats of a cement waterproofing paint such as Thoroseal into the walls.

If water leaks through a crack or hole, chip out the opening with a cold chisel; blow out the crumbs; and pack in a mixture of one part cement and two parts sand. If the crack leaks continuously, substitute quick-setting hydraulic cement for the cement-sand mix. Cracks in the joint between a wall and the floor can be filled, if dry, with asphalt roofing cement. Use hydraulic cement if they are wet.

To clean floor. Sprinkle with floor-sweeping compound—a dry, sawdustlike material—and sweep with a broom. Compound can be reused.

BLANKETS

Routine maintenance. If blankets have been used regularly, wash or dry-clean them once a year before putting them away. If they have been used infrequently (in a guest room, for example), you may never really need to clean them; but they will be more attractive if you do.

Replace bindings when they become threadbare or torn. Store woolen blankets in tight polyethylene bags with naphthalene or paradichlorobenzene flakes.

To launder blankets in automatic equipment. Woolen and electric blankets must be handled in the following way. Other blankets are best handled in the same way, too.

Use a light-duty detergent. The water temperature should not exceed 100 degrees. Wash only one blanket at a time. Pretreat heavily soiled bindings and spots with a paste of the

147

detergent you plan to use. Wash in your automatic washer for two minutes at the slowest speed. Spin at normal speed. Rinse in warm or cold water.

Dry one blanket at a time. Set the automatic-dryer timer for twenty to twenty-five minutes. Put a half-dozen large Turkish towels in the drum, and let them heat for five minutes. Then put the blanket in the drum with the towels and let it tumble gently until the cycle ends. Remove it at once (it should feel slightly damp); stretch it carefully to its original dimensions, and allow it to air-dry flat on a bed or on a line. Finally, press bindings with a warm iron.

BLENDERS

Routine maintenance. Wash well with warm detergent solution after each use. Dry carefully and turn the impeller several times to keep it from sticking.

BRASS

To clean. Rub with brass polish until every vestige of dirt and polish is removed (nothing comes off on a clean rag). Brass plate is cleaned the same way. However, if an article is lacquered, simply wash with a detergent solution.

If lacquer wears off. Remove the remaining lacquer with lacquer thinner. Clean and rinse well. Then apply one or two new coats of lacquer with an aerosol. (Note that lacquered brass is not so lustrous as unfinished brass that is simply polished well.)

BRICK

See also exterior walls, masonry.

To clean. Scrub with a strong detergent solution, then rinse. If dirt is thick and stubborn, as on a house in an industrial city, use a power washer which blasts the bricks with streams of cold water under high pressure. Small units of this type are sold by Sears, Montgomery Ward, etc.

To remove efflorescence. Try scrubbing with water and a wire brush. If this doesn't work, saturate the brick with water; then scrub with one part hydrochloric acid mixed with nine parts water. Use a fiber brush only. Rinse thoroughly within ten minutes.

To remove green or greenish-brown vanadium stains. Mix one 12-ounce can of sodium hydroxide (Drano) in a quart of water and apply it liberally to the stains with a paintbrush. Let it stand for three days; then wash off the white salt on the bricks with water.

To remove oily, brown manganese stains on mortar joints between bricks. Brush or spray with Brick Klenz according to manufacturer's directions. The alternative is to spray with one part 80 per cent acetic acid, one part 30 per cent hydrogen peroxide and six parts water; then rinse when stains disappear. Stains may reappear within a few days after the latter treatment, however.

To remove iron stains. Brush with one pound oxalic acid in one gallon water.

To remove green copper stains. Make a thick paste of one part ammonium chloride, four parts talc and a little household ammonia. Spread a thick layer over the stain and let it dry. Then scrape off. Make repeat applications as necessary.

To remove smoke stains. Scrub with water and a household cleanser. If this doesn't work, make a thick paste of talc and trichloroethylene; spread on the stains; allow to dry; then scrape off. Make repeat applications as necessary.

To remove grease, oil and tar stains. Apply an emulsifier like those used in service stations (Big Red or ND-150, for example). Or apply a poultice as for smoke stains.

To remove moss and algae, which stain bricks green. Brush bricks with ammonium sulfamate (Ammate) solution recommended by the manufacturer. Or wash with vinegar. Allow to set for several days. Then remove dead growth with a wire brush. Note that ammonium sulfamate will also kill any other vegetation it touches.

To remove paint. Take off as much as possible with a putty knife and steel wool. Remove the remainder with paint remover.

BRONZE

Treat like brass (which see).

BRUSHED CHROME

Note. Brushed chrome is a type of stainless steel often used on major appliances.

Routine maintenance. Clean as necessary with rubbing alcohol or with a solution of two tablespoons water softener, such as Calgon, in a quart of warm water. Rub briskly to dry. Avoid using soap or detergent because they leave streaks. However, if a chrome surface is very dirty or greasy, you must first wash with a mild detergent solution and then wipe with alcohol or water softener.

CABINETS, KITCHEN

Routine maintenance. Scrub off fingerprints, grease and food splatters regularly with a mild detergent solution. If cabinets are wood or metal, substitute for the detergent—at about every third or fourth application—a white, liquid cleaning wax made for use on appliances.

Vacuum and wash insides of cabinets and drawers used for food storage about every six months to keep mice and insects from becoming interested.

CABINETS, MEDICINE

Routine maintenance. Wash enameled bottom of cabinet frequently to prevent deterioration of the paint by medicines, etc., that have spilled. Wash glass, plastic and chrome-steel shelves at least once a year. Brush or vacuum dirt out of channels in which doors slide once a year.

CAN OPENERS, ELECTRIC

Routine maintenance. Remove magnet and cutter head every three to six months, depending on how much the can opener is used, and clean them in a strong detergent solution. At the same time, wash the entire can opener. When reassembling cutter head, be sure to screw it on tight.

CARPETS

Routine maintenance. For thorough cleaning, use a vacuum cleaner with a revolving brush. For light cleaning, you can use a vacuum that has suction only, an electric broom or a carpet sweeper. Shampooing is best done with a liquid applied according to manufacturer's directions.

In a room that is rarely occupied, thorough-clean the carpet only when dusting the furniture. Shampooing or professional cleaning is rarely necessary.

In a room with average traffic, thorough-clean the carpet once a week and shampoo it once a year.

In a room with heavy traffic, light-clean the carpet twice a week and thorough-clean it once. Shampoo it twice at six-month intervals and have it professionally cleaned at the end of eighteen months; then repeat the cycle.

In a room with heavy traffic and a frequently used outside door, thorough-clean the carpet three times a week. Alternate shampooing and professional cleaning at six-month intervals.

In a kitchen, thorough-clean the carpet every day. Shampoo it twice at four-month intervals, and have it professionally cleaned at the end of every year.

Cut off tufts that protrude above the carpet surface.

If possible, turn the carpet once a year so that it does not wear excessively in one spot.

To clean small cotton rugs. Vacuum as necessary. Wash for six minutes in your washing machine when rugs begin to show soil. Use hot water for colorfast rugs; warm water for non-colorfast rugs. Rinse waters should be warm and cold respectively. Rugs can then be dried in an automatic dryer.

To clean acrylic-fiber throw rugs. Vacuum as necessary. Wash and rinse in warm water. Then dry in an automatic dryer at the low-temperature setting for about twenty to thirty minutes. Remove rug before it is completely dry, shake and lay it out flat to dry. (If acrylic-fiber rugs are dryed completely in a dryer, the fibers are likely to bend over and mat.)

To clean grass and straw rugs. Vacuum as necessary. Lift rugs and vacuum floor underneath every two or three months. Sponge rugs with mild detergent solution every six months.

To remove dents in pile. If they don't disappear when brushed, hold a steam iron just above them and apply steam.

To remove stains. Go to work on them at once. The National Institute of Rug Cleaning's laboratories report that 90 per cent of all liquids can be removed if immediate action is taken. Scrape up any solid matter, and blot up as much moisture as possible with clean white cloths. Then, working from the edges of the stain inward, blot the stain with the required cleaning agent. Avoid rubbing, if you can, and don't get the carpet any wetter than necessary. Sponge up the excess moisture. Then cover with a thick layer of white cloth or facial tissue, weight down and allow the cleaned area to dry for six hours.

Alcohol, animal urine, beer, bleach, coffee, mustard, soot, syrup, tea, wine. Clean with one teaspoon mild laundry detergent in a half pint lukewarm water. Rinse with one part white vinegar and two parts lukewarm water.

Butter, cologne, grease, metal polish. Clean with dry-cleaning fluid. Rinse with one teaspoon mild laundry detergent in a half pint lukewarm water. Then rinse with one part white vinegar and two parts lukewarm water.

Cellulose cement, chewing gum, cosmetics, fruit and fruit juices, oils, ointment, shoe polish. Clean with dry-cleaning fluid. Wash with one teaspoon mild laundry detergent in a half pint lukewarm water. Then apply one tablespoon ammonia in three-quarters cup water. Finally rinse with one part white vinegar and two parts lukewarm water.

Blood, candy, chocolate, egg, glue, ice cream, milk, soft drinks, vomit and excrement. Follow second, third and fourth steps listed immediately above. If greasy stains persist after this treatment, apply dry-cleaning fluid.

Tar. Clean with dry-cleaning fluid.

Wax. Clean with dry-cleaning fluid. Candle wax should first be scraped up carefully with a blunt knife.

CHIMNEYS

Routine maintenance. Check annually for cracks and crumbling mortar, and repoint as necessary with one part cement and two parts sand. Make sure flashing is secure and sound. Have flues cleaned every other year unless you use your fireplaces a great deal, in which case annual cleaning is called

Depending on the amount of use, carpets should be professionally cleaned every 12 to 18 months. The cleaning is best done at the cleaning establishment but can be done in the home. (National Institute of Rug Cleaning)

for. Have smoke pipe from oil furnace and water heater to chimney cleaned every year.

CHROME-PLATED STEEL

See also brushed chrome.

Routine maintenance. Clean as necessary with detergent solution. If surface is scratched, apply a chrome cleaner and chrome protector from an auto-supply store.

To remove stubborn stains, baked-on food and carbon. Clean as well as possible with detergent solution. Then brush on a powerful grease and carbon remover, such as It, and allow to stand for thirty minutes to an hour—or overnight in the case of very thick deposits. Then agitate the remover and wash it off with cold water.

COFFEEMAKERS

Routine maintenance. Wash, rinse and dry thoroughly after every use. Scrub with household cleanser to remove accumulated coffee-oil stains. To clean exterior, see chrome-plated steel or aluminum.

CONCRETE

To remove oil and grease stains. If stain is new, soak up as much of the oil as possible with paper towels; cover it with a ½-inch layer of dry cement or patching plaster for about twenty-four hours; then sweep up the cement and scrub the stain with a strong detergent solution. A simpler alternative—especially good in garages—is to toss a product such as Zorbal or Oil-Dri (sold by auto-supply stores) on the stain; allow it to soak up the oil, and then sweep up.

Treat old stains with one of the cleaners used in service stations and sold by auto-supply stores.

To remove rust stains. Pour a phosphoric acid cleaner such as Rust-Oleum Surfa-Etch on the stain and scrub with a bristle brush. Rinse well.

To remove smoke stains. Scrub with a household cleanser and water. If stain persists, make a thick paste of talc and

154

trichloroethylene; spread it on the stain and allow to dry; then scrape off. Make repeat applications as necessary.

To remove paint stains. Use a paint remover.

COPPER

To remove stains and tarnish. Clean with a brass polish. If stains persist, rub with very fine steel wool or emery cloth.

If lacquer wears off. Remove the remaining lacquer with lacquer thinner. Clean metal thoroughly. Then spray on one or two new coats of lacquer.

CORK

To remove stains. Wash with a detergent solution. If this doesn't work, sand the cork lightly with medium sandpaper; finish with fine sandpaper. Note, however, that cork is easily and deeply stained by many things, so cleaning may be impossible. To protect against this eventuality, you can seal it with two or three coats of shellac thinned 50-50 with denatured alcohol.

CURTAINS AND DRAPERIES

Routine maintenance. Vacuum curtains and draperies every month to six months depending on the amount of dust and dirt in the air. Wash or dry-clean according to manufacturer's directions as soon as they show signs of embedded soil, because dirt and grease shorten the life of fabrics and also give the hangings an unpleasant odor. (If you are not sure curtains are machine-washable, play safe and wash them by hand.) If possible, at the time of washing, alternate curtains and draperies between sunny and shady windows to lengthen the life of the fabric and make fading more uniform.

In machine-washing curtains, wash cottons and linens in hot water with a heavy-duty detergent; rayons, acetates and permanent-press in warm water with a light-duty detergent. Permanent-press fabrics should be spun dry in the washer at slow speed, and removed from the tub as soon as the spin stops. If your washer lacks a slow spin speed, spin curtains at high speed for only two or three minutes and remove them at once.

Most curtains and draperies can also be dried in an automatic dryer. Use low temperature for all except cottons and linens. Remove from the dryer while the curtains are still slightly damp. For permanent-press fabrics, the dryer should have a cool-down period at the end of the cycle. The curtains should then be removed immediately from the drum.

DISHWASHERS

To clean. Clean exterior enamel with detergent solution or white, liquid cleaning wax. Clean exterior brushed-chrome panels with two tablespoons water softener dissolved in warm water or with rubbing alcohol.

If a white film builds up in dishwasher tub because your water is hard, remove it with a mild cleansing powder; or place a bowl with two cups white vinegar in the bottom rack and run the dishwasher through its regular cycle. (Don't use this vinegar wash more than once a month, however.)

To maintain a wood top on a portable dishwasher. After washing top or spilling water on it, dry it well. If water stains appear, rub them with mineral oil. If top becomes very dirty, stained or scratched, go over it with fine steel wool or sandpaper, and then rub it with mineral oil.

DOORS

Routine maintenance. Wash off fingerprints and other dirt with mild detergent solution. Apply a self-polishing cleaner wax of the type used on floors to stained doors every four months to protect the finish. Dust interior paneled doors every couple of months; exterior doors every month. Remove dirt and sand from the floor track of sliding glass doors every week. Oil locks and latches sparingly once a year. Clean out dirt that collects in swinging-door hinges once a year, and apply oil or powdered graphite.

Brush or vacuum dust and sand out of flexible-metal weather stripping at the base of exterior doors every month. Inspect all weather stripping in the autumn and repair as necessary.

To remove heel and scuff marks. Clean with a strong detergent such as Fantastik. Then rewax the doors if they have a clear finish.

DOORS, GARAGE

Routine maintenance. Oil all moving parts every six months. Check wood doors with inset panels to make sure cracks have not developed between the panels and the frame. Fill any cracks with calking compound or putty. Adjust springs when necessary to permit easy opening of doors and to keep them from coming down with a bang.

DOORSILLS

Routine maintenance. Because the sills are exposed to weather and heavy traffic, they must be repainted or revarnished about every six months if you want them to look decent. A sound finish also helps to keep moisture out of the wood and thus minimizes discoloring and decay.

DRYERS

Routine maintenance. Clean out lint trap after every use. Vacuum behind lint trap and under and behind dryer cabinet every six months. Wipe out dryer drum once a month to remove excess lint. At the same time, remove any metal articles such as bobby pins and nails that you find sticking through the holes in the drum. Clean out exhaust duct once a year by pushing your vacuum-cleaner hose into it through the exterior exhaust cap. Clean dryer top and control panel with a damp cloth or mild detergent solution every month. Apply white, liquid cleaning wax every two or three months to the front and sides.

ELECTRIC BLANKETS

See blankets. Electric blankets should be washed. They can also be dry-cleaned if the proper cleaning fluids are used; but inasmuch as some cleaning fluids will ruin the wiring insulation, it is better not to take a chance.

ELECTRIC CORDS

Routine maintenance. Examine cords yearly for worn spots

and cracks, and replace those found to be defective. Breaks are most likely to occur where a cord enters a plug and where the base of a lamp or a piece of furniture may rest on the cord. Cords that feel very stiff should be discarded even though they show no signs of wear, because you can never tell when they will crack.

To protect Christmas tree lights. Because mice sometimes chew on the insulation, store cords in a tight closet or wrap them in aluminum foil.

EXTERIOR WALLS—ALL TYPES

To keep watertight. Inspect calked joints every fall. Scrape out loose calking and replace with new, long-life calking (see page 51). Calk new cracks that have opened between siding and window- or doorframes, chimneys, etc. Inspect flashing over windows and doors.

To prevent termite damage. Inspect foundation walls outside and, if possible, inside once a year for earthen tubes extending up from the ground. Remove any tubes you find. Pull soil away from walls if it is within six inches of the siding. Call in an exterminator to treat the soil with chlordane if termites are in evidence.

To clean. Hosing down the walls once a year and scrubbing off stubborn dirt with a stiff broom or bristle brush usually takes care of most of the dirt that accumulates. (It also helps to even up the appearance of wood and plywood walls that are allowed to weather naturally.) But in unusually dirty atmospheres, you may have to scrub the walls with a mild detergent; and in extreme cases, you may need to use a high-pressure power washer.

Make sure that gutters are clean and sound; if not, they may cause soiling and staining of the siding below.

To remove mildew. Scrub with a strong detergent solution to which a little chlorine bleach has been added. If mildew is stubborn, add about two-thirds cup trisodium phosphate to a solution containing one-third cup detergent, one quart bleach and three quarts water.

EXTERIOR WALLS, ASBESTOS-CEMENT

To remove copper stains. Scrub with an abrasive household cleanser. If stains persist, brush white vinegar on the stains and then rinse with water.

To remove iron stains. Scrub with an abrasive household cleaner. Brush with one pound oxalic acid in one gallon water if stains persist.

To remove fungus growth. Scrub with an abrasive household cleanser. If necessary, saturate the growth with one part copper sulfate in ten parts hot water.

To prevent leakage caused by a broken shingle. Insert a piece of aluminum flashing metal under the shingle. The top of the metal should extend up beyond the butt of the shingle in the next course above. (This should be considered a temporary maintenance measure only.)

EXTERIOR WALLS, MASONRY

Routine maintenance. Inspect mortar joints every fall; and wherever cement is crumbling or cracked, scrape it out and repoint with one part cement and two parts sand or with prepared vinyl-concrete patching cement.

To stop leaks. If leaks are not attributed to cracks, you may assume that water is soaking into the masonry blocks and mortar and somehow forcing its way through to the interior surfaces. The best way to prevent such leakage is to waterproof the walls all over with a Portland cement paint; but this means that you must from time to time take on the new job of refinishing the walls to preserve an attractive finish. The alternative is to apply a solvent-based, transparent, colorless waterproofer containing a silicone. This, however, does not actually waterproof the wall but merely dampproofs it. The finish needs to be reapplied every five years.

To remove stains. See brick.

EXTERIOR WALLS, STUCCO

To stop leaks. Hairline cracks can be sealed by brushing on Portland cement paint. If cracks are large, cut them open with a cold chisel, clean out the crumbs and fill with mortar

159

made of one part cement, three parts sand and one-tenth part hydrated lime. Or fill with a prepared vinyl-concrete patching cement.

EXTERIOR WALLS, WOOD AND PLYWOOD

Routine maintenance. The average life of a good quality white exterior paint is four years; of a medium-color paint, five years; of a dark paint, six years. You should therefore repaint your house every four, five or six years according to its color. If you repaint more often than this, you do not give the old paint time to weather sufficiently; and the new paint may not stick to it well. If you repaint less often, the old paint deteriorates to a point where you must do a lot of scraping, sanding and priming before applying new paint.

Wood finished with an opaque stain should be restained every six to eight years, depending on the appearance of the walls. If a transparent stain is used, restain the walls every three to five years.

Prefinished plywood may go for years without requiring paint. And of course, wood and plywood that are allowed to weather naturally never need painting. There is, however, some tendency for unfinished boards and shingles to cup or split. These should be secured with galvanized nails.

To prevent leaks when shingles break. See exterior walls, asbestos-cement.

FANS

Routine maintenance. Clean thoroughly at the end of the summer; store wrapped in polyethylene or some other kind of protective cover; oil in the spring.

FANS, VENTILATING

Routine maintenance. Remove interior and exterior covers, vacuum the covers and fan assembly thoroughly and then clean with a strong detergent solution. Fans installed close to the kitchen range will require cleaning every three months at least; those far away, once a year. Much depends on how much deep-fat frying you do.

If the fan is installed in a hood over the range, clean the bottom (metal) filter at least monthly. Agitate it in a hot detergent solution and scrub lightly with a soft kitchen brush. Then rinse and shake dry.

Fiberglass filters in hood fans can also be cleaned in a detergent solution, but it's an uncertain job. Better replace them with new filters. Charcoal filters also need to be replaced. The frequency of replacement depends on how greasy filters get. Just don't continue to use them when they are clogged so badly that fan efficiency is reduced.

Oil fan motor as directed by the manufacturer.

FENCES

Routine maintenance. Hose off dirt once a year. Pull dirt, leaves and other debris away from the bottoms of wooden pickets and rails. Renail or screw loose joints. If fence posts are wobbly, firm the soil around them with a tamper. (Wobbly posts often invite children to make them even more wobbly.) Remove rust from iron fences once a year; then prime and repaint the spots. Repaint the entire fence—iron or wood— every four years.

FIREPLACES

Routine maintenance. Sweep the hearth after you have a fire. Remove all ashes when they are a couple of inches deep in the center of the fireplace. (If the wind blows down the chimney, ashes should be removed as soon as a fire is dead; otherwise they will be scattered throughout the room.)

Remove smoke and other stains as they appear on the fireplace breast, hearth and mantel. See brick; marble; tile, ceramic; floors, wood.

To clean brass andirons, fenders and tools. See brass. Dust iron andirons, etc., when you dust the furniture, and wash them in detergent solution once a year.

FLOORS, BRICK

Routine maintenance. If floor is not finished, the bricks should be vacuumed every other day to get up dirt and brick

161

dust which tracks through the house. Even if the floor has a finish, it needs to be vacuumed once or twice a week to pick up lint and dirt that clings to it.

If brick is finished and waxed with a buffable liquid wax (the best kind to use), buff the floor every six to eight weeks and rewax every four to six months, depending on the traffic.

Wash an unfinished brick floor that is laid in mortar every two or six months. A finished brick floor laid in mortar should be damp-mopped only—and only if it looks very soiled. Bricks that are laid dry should always be finished. Clean with a damp mop.

To remove stains. See bricks if the floor is unfinished. See floors, wood if the brick is finished and waxed. Substances that seep into pores of bricks must be removed with a scrub brush.

FLOORS, CERAMIC-TILE

See tile, ceramic.

FLOORS, CONCRETE

Routine maintenance. Sweep daily and vacuum once a week to get up dirt that eludes your broom. If the floor gets unusually dirty and dusty, as in a basement, sweep it occasionally with a sweeping compound. Save the compound after it is picked up in your dustpan and use it again. When the floor eventually becomes too dirty to bear, scrub it with water and possibly a detergent.

To remove stains. See concrete.

FLOORS, FLAGSTONE AND SLATE

Routine maintenance. Whether the floor is finished or not, vacuum it once or twice a week. Wash an unfinished floor with mild detergent solution or plain water every six months. Damp-mop a finished floor with a mild detergent solution when it becomes soiled. If floor is finished, apply a buffable liquid wax every four to six months; and between times, buff the floor every six to eight weeks.

To remove stains. Follow directions for bricks (which see)

162

if the floor is unfinished. See floors, wood if the brick is finished and waxed.

FLOORS, MARBLE

Routine maintenance. Dry-mop every third day of the week and vacuum every seventh. When floor gets dirty, wash it with a marble cleaner such as that made by Vermarco; sponge up dirty water promptly, and rinse well. To help prevent staining, apply a penetrating, colorless sealer, such as Tri-Seal, every four months after the floor is washed. After this has set for thirty minutes, wipe up the excess and buff with an electric polisher.

To remove small scratches. Rub with very, very fine sandpaper. Then wet the surface with water, dip a damp cloth in a little tin oxide powder, and rub until the shine returns.

To remove stains. See marble.

FLOORS, QUARRY-TILE

Routine maintenance. Vacuum once or twice a week. Wash with mild detergent solution every three or four months. If grouted joints become dirty, scrub with a bathroom-tile cleaner, such as Afta.

To remove stains. Almost all staining agents can be wiped from the tiles with water or detergent solution. But for stubborn stains, see tile, ceramic.

FLOORS, RESILIENT

Routine maintenance. This is one of the homemaker's hardest jobs—not because resilient flooring is difficult to maintain but because she usually goes about it in the wrong way. Her principal mistakes: She applies too much wax or, instead of wax, she applies some sort of hard finish, such as lacquer, which turns yellow, wears unevenly and cannot be removed without damage to the flooring.

The main idea in maintaining a resilient floor is to apply only enough wax—never anything else—to protect the floor, but not enough to build up into a thick film that must eventually be stripped off completely. Stripping is the worst job in floor care.

163

Starting with a new or absolutely clean floor, here is the best procedure to follow:

Apply a self-polishing water-based wax or—more work but more durable—a buffable water-based wax.

Sweep or vacuum the floor daily to pick up dust and dirt that would otherwise become embedded in the wax coating. Remove stains as they occur (see below).

Damp-mop with water or a very mild detergent solution about once a week.

Wet-mop with mild detergent solution once a month. Do not flood the floor with water; use just enough to wet it. Scrub stains well. Sponge up whatever moisture remains and rinse (always rinse despite what detergent makers say) with clear water. Sponge up the residue as much as possible and allow the floor to dry.

Then apply self-polishing water-based wax to the floor area *which is not overhung by cabinets, appliances and tables that are rarely moved and rarely used.* (In other words, don't wax floor areas that are not regularly walked on or scuffed; otherwise they will become coated with so much wax that they will not match the rest of the floor. Such areas need waxing only about once a year.)

(If you have an electric floor polisher, using a buffable self-polishing wax will help to maintain the appearance of the floor; and you may not need to wash it so often. But of course you must bring out the polisher every now and then.)

When at last the floor begins to look yellow or uneven or does not respond to washing and rewaxing, it probably should be stripped. To make sure this is necessary, apply a little stripping solution to a small out-of-the-way area and compare its appearance with the rest of the floor.

To strip an entire floor, use a prepared, one-step wax remover. Apply to a one-yard-square area and let stand for about three minutes; then scrub vigorously with a stiff brush, very fine steel wool or an electric floor scrubber. When the wax is loosened, take it up with a mop and proceed to another area. When the entire floor has been stripped, rinse it with clear water. Apply additional wax remover to any areas that still appear dull. Then dry thoroughly and apply self-polishing wax—one coat on reasonably new floors; two coats on old. The wax coats should be thin and even.

To remove excess wax from small areas, simply rub with fine steel wool dipped in wax remover. Do not, however, use steel wool at any time on printed resilient flooring materials.

To remove stains. The trick here is to remove the stain without removing any more wax than necessary. To do this, limit your scrubbing to the stain itself; and don't use overly powerful solvents.

Start out with a mild detergent solution. If stain persists, rub with a damp cloth dipped in white, liquid cleaning wax made for appliances. This will definitely remove heel marks, grease, tar, lipstick, soot, crayon, food stains and shoe polish. If stain still persists, rub with a damp cloth dipped in abrasive household cleanser. If necessary, use fine steel wool also.

To remove nail polish, nail-polish remover and other solvents. Wipe up immediately, if possible. If material hardens, scrape it off carefully with a knife. Then go over spot with fine steel wool and abrasive cleanser.

To remove burns. Rub with fine steel wool and abrasive cleanser.

To remove chewing gum. Scrape the flooring as clean as possible with a dull knife. Then rub with very, very little dry-cleaning fluid.

FLOORS—SEAMLESS FLOORING

Routine maintenance. Dry-mop every three days; vacuum once a week. When dirty, clean with a damp mop and mild detergent solution.

Seamless floors made of acrylic should be reglazed about every six months to restore their gloss. Those made of urethane need reglazing every three to five years. Resurfacing in heavy-traffic areas is also required—but less frequently.

Epoxy floors are never reglazed, but may need to be resurfaced in traffic areas at widely spaced intervals.

Glaze is applied to a clean floor with a roller. You can do the job. But resurfacing calls for professional help.

To remove stains. Seamless flooring is very resistant to staining and generally can be cleaned simply with water or a mild detergent solution. But if stains prove difficult, follow directions for floors, resilient.

FLOORS, TERRAZZO

Routine maintenance. Alternate dry-mopping and vacuuming at three- to four-day intervals. When floor becomes dirty, dissolve ½ cup neutral liquid cleaner such as Vermarco marble cleaner in 1½ gallons water; mop this liberally onto the floor; allow to stand for several minutes but not long enough for the water to evaporate; then take up with a sponge or mop. Rinse thoroughly and allow to dry. Then, if you have an electric floor polisher, buff the floor to bring out its beauty and add to its sheen. To minimize staining of the floor by grease, alkalies, etc., apply a penetrating, colorless sealer, such as Tri-Seal, every six months after the floor is washed and dried but before it is buffed.

To remove stains. Most staining agents can be wiped up with water. For other stains, see floors, concrete.

FLOORS, WOOD

Routine maintenance. Wood floors should be waxed with paste wax or buffable liquid wax to start. Thereafter, dry-mop or vacuum the floors to remove grit and dust. In heavily traveled areas, this may be necessary every day or two; in more lightly traveled areas, only once a week or even less often.

As a floor begins to show fine scratches or dirt, buff with an electric floor polisher. About every four months, or when the floor becomes very tired-looking, apply a thin coat of buffable liquid wax or a self-polishing cleaner wax. Either material will clean and polish the floor. The buffable wax, however, must be polished; but to compensate for this deficiency, it is more durable than the cleaner wax.

If wood floors are not overwaxed, they should never build up a coating that requires complete removal. If complete removal is necessary, do not use water or water-based stripping compounds like those used on resilient floors, since such

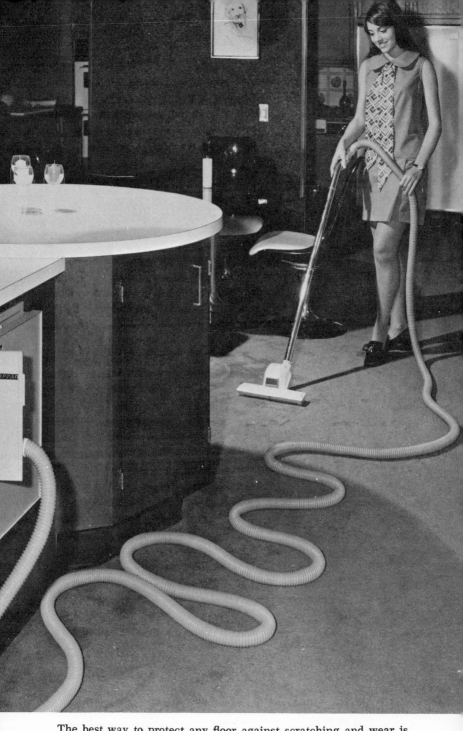

The best way to protect any floor against scratching and wear is to vacuum it regularly. A built-in vacuum cleaning system such as this is desirable because it saves work as noted on page 43.

treatment will damage the wood. Use naphtha and scrub with coarse rags.

An important routine step in wood-floor maintenance is to keep loose boards nailed down tight. If the old nails do not hold, drill a very small hole through the loose board at an angle and drive in four-inch cement-coated finishing nails. Countersink the head and cover with plastic wood.

If boards squeak, nail them down in the same way.

If wood plugs in a "pegged" wide-board floor come loose, reset them with white wood glue.

To remove burns. Scrape the charred spot very carefully along the grain with a knife. Then smooth with sandpaper, clean with naphtha and apply stain and finish to match the surrounding wood.

To remove dents. Place a damp cloth on the dent. Turn a bottle cap upside down directly over the dent. Heat the cap for brief periods with a warm iron.

To conceal scratches. Rub with paste wax. Sometimes scratches in a floor with a gym-seal finish can be rubbed out with turpentine. Similar scratches in shellac can be rubbed out with alcohol. The only way to remove deep scratches is to sand down the area around them thoroughly or to fill the scratches with a melted shellac stick of the proper color.

To remove stains. Alcohol spots on shellac. Even out with very fine steel wool. Then brush on new shellac diluted 50-50 with denatured alcohol. Rub down well with fine steel wool; and apply a second coat of diluted shellac and rub down again.

Alcohol spots on other finishes. Rub with a rag dipped in salad oil and rottenstone.

Water spots. Dip a rag in salad oil, then in cigarette ashes and rub well. If stain persists, daub camphorated oil on the spot and allow to stand for thirty minutes. Then rub with rottenstone and oil.

Water spots on bare wood. If water is allowed to stand too long on bare wood, it will eventually stain the wood almost black. Similar black spots occur on finished wood also. Removal in either case is impossible except by deep sanding.

The only alternative is to try to bleach the stain with a commercial bleach.

Paint spots. Carefully scrape up what you can with a knife. Then rub with rottenstone and oil.

Candle wax. Remove as much as possible with a dull knife and take off what's left with naphtha.

Crayon and lipstick. Remove with white, liquid cleaning wax used for kitchen appliances.

Heel marks. Rub with white, liquid cleaning wax. If marks persist, use fine steel wool in addition.

FREEZERS

Routine maintenance. Clean exterior enamel frequently—especially around the handle—with mild detergent solution or white, liquid cleaning wax. Clean door gasket with detergent solution every three months. If you have a no-frost model, defrosting is automatic; but the drain pan in the very bottom of the freezer should be removed and washed every four to six months. If you have a manual-defrost model, defrost it every six months—or every four months if you use the freezer frequently. Remove food packages, turn off the freezer and open the door until all ice has melted. Then wash the interior with two tablespoons baking soda in a quart of water.

FRYING PANS, ELECTRIC

Routine maintenance. After cooking, before pouring fat from the pan, tear off a paper towel and hold it in one hand. Then pour the fat into the grease can. Hold the pan almost vertical so that the fat will not curl down around the sides and under the bottom of the pan. As soon as the last of the fat is gone, wipe the outside of the pan at the pouring corner with the paper towel. By following this simple procedure, you will help to reduce the build-up of grease and carbon on the bottom of the pan.

Do not put the pan in water until it has cooled somewhat: it may warp, otherwise. When washing, scrub the bottom of the pan as well as the inside. Use soap, detergent or cleaning powder.

169

Despite these precautions, the bottom of the pan will probably become badly soiled and encrusted with grease and carbon (which melt onto the kitchen counter when the pan is in use). To get this off, apply a strong grease and carbon remover such as It to the pan bottom every three to six months. Let it stand for thirty to sixty minutes—even longer if the carbon build-up is thick. Then agitate it well and rinse thoroughly in cold water.

FURNITURE, METAL

Routine maintenance. Dust as necessary. Wash surfaces that are touched by hands with mild detergent solution every two or three months or, better, clean with a white, liquid cleaning wax. Touch up bare spots caused by chipping and scratching as you discover them. Remove products of corrosion if they appear, and refinish. On chrome, clean scratches with a chrome cleaner and spray on a chrome protector.

FURNITURE, RUSH, WICKER, RATTAN, REED, BAMBOO

Routine maintenance. Vacuum as necessary to remove dust, food particles, etc. Remove spills and stains by sponging with detergent solution or cleaning fluid, according to the type of stain.

To keep bindings from unraveling. When this type of material (rush, wicker, etc.) is woven, a break in one strip does not as a rule set off a chain reaction marked by breakage of other strips. But when a strip is used to bind together several members of the furniture piece (as when a strip of bamboo is used to bind a leg and rung of a chair), a break in the strip is often followed by the unraveling and loss of the entire strip. To prevent this, glue down the strip as soon as you notice it is cracked or completely broken. Driving a small brad through it into the wood beneath helps further to secure it.

FURNITURE, UPHOLSTERED

Routine maintenance. Whether upholstery is treated with a fabric protector or not, vacuum furniture every two to four weeks to remove dust and dirt. Shampoo fabrics which can

170

withstand such treatment once a year or more often if they become dirty in the interim. Turn loose cushions occasionally. About once a year remove slipcovers and zippered permanent covers and either wash them or send them to a dry cleaner.

Clean leather upholstery with a leather cleaner and conditioner every three months. Use a vinyl cleaner every four to six months on vinyl upholstery.

To remove stains. Always test the cleaning agent on an inconspicuous area before working on the stain. Vacuum upholstery thoroughly. Use as little liquid as possible; and if the first application does not remove the stain, make repeat applications.

Alcohol. Sponge with water.

Candle wax. Scrape with a dull knife. Then apply cleaning fluid.

Chewing gum. Remove as much as possible with a dull knife. Then, working from the edges in, loosen the gum bit by bit with cleaning fluid, and scrape it off.

Food stains. Sponge with water; blot up as much as possible, and allow to dry. If stain persists, food probably contained grease; so apply cleaning fluid.

Urine. Sponge with water.

FURNITURE, WOOD

Routine maintenance. Dust as necessary. Remove hand marks, smudges, dirt, grease, etc., as they appear, with a sponge wrung out in mild detergent solution. Rinse well. Polish furniture surfaces which are not exposed to wear every four to six months with furniture polish. Use this sparingly and buff it well with a dry cloth. Surfaces that are exposed to hard wear and are often touched by hands—tabletops, chair arms and drawer fronts, for example—should be polished with a good liquid or paste wax. The frequency of waxing varies from about every two months for tabletops to every four months for drawer fronts. Buffing with an electric polisher can be substituted for every other new wax application.

At least once a year, examine glued joints and reglue any that are loose. Chairs particularly need attention because they are much more easily broken—sometimes beyond repair—when the joints are unsound. Reglue loose veneer at the same time.

To keep drawers from sticking in summer. In late winter, rub the surfaces that habitually bind with paraffin. This is not a perfect answer but will help. See page 133.

To remove heat marks. Rub with camphorated oil and dry at once. If marks persist or surface is roughened, rub with a cloth dipped in salad oil and rottenstone.

To remove burns, dents, stains. See floors, wood.

To remove scratches. On a clear finish, rub with paste wax or the meat of a nut. Deep scratches can be filled with a colored-wax stick or touched up with stain and finish to match the surrounding area. On painted furniture, touch up with paint.

GATES

Routine maintenance. Treat like fences (which see). In addition, oil hinges once a year at least.

GUTTERS AND LEADERS

Routine maintenance. Clean at least twice a year—in late fall after the leaves are down but before the temperature drops permanently below freezing, and in late spring after petals fall. If you need a heating cable to keep your gutters and leaders open during the winter (see page 132), inspect the installation in the fall. At the same time replace broken gutter hanger straps; straighten out bends; plug leaks.

If gutters are galvanized steel or wood, brush the troughs every two years with asphalt roof coating or polysulfide rubber.

HEATING SYSTEMS

Routine maintenance. Clean or replace filters in a warm-air system every two to three months, depending on the type of air-cleaning device you have. Remove lime deposits and dirt from humidifiers every two to three months. Oil motors if and as called for by the manufacturer. Vent radiators in a hot-water system every fall. Inspect and if necessary clean steam valves in gasoline every other fall. Have oil burner cleaned and serviced by your oil dealer every summer or fall. Flues for oil-fired heating systems should also be cleaned annually.

To clean radiators. Clean every three months at least with the crevice tool of your vacuum cleaner. If dust sticks between the tubes of a radiator, try getting it off with a radiator or bottle brush. If this doesn't work, place newspapers under the radiator and clean it with a brush dipped in detergent solution.

To keep a steam radiator from hammering. This happens when water returning from the radiator to the boiler is trapped in the pipe. To correct, raise the radiator off the floor on wood blocks so that the pipe slants toward the boiler.

To clean warm-air registers. Use a vacuum cleaner. But you should not have to do this job more than once a year—if that—if you clean the furnace filter regularly.

INTERIOR WALLS—CLEAR-FINISHED WOOD PANELING

Routine maintenance. Dust with a vacuum cleaner once a year (but much more often if the paneling has insets). Remove smudges from around light switches, etc., with a mild detergent solution once a month; and clean with white, liquid cleaning wax every third month. Remove scuff marks with a strong detergent such as Fantastik. Apply furniture polish every couple of years to the entire wall surface to clean and bring out the full beauty of the wood.

INTERIOR WALLS, GYPSUM-BOARD

Routine maintenance. Make a close visual inspection of the walls and ceilings every six months for bumps that indicate the nails holding the wallboards have popped loose. Drive the nails back into the studs with a hammer; and to prevent the nails from popping loose again, drive one ring-grooved nail alongside. Fill the depressions made by your hammer with spackle or gypsum-board cement. Then paint.

INTERIOR WALLS—PAINTED OR STAINED

Routine maintenance. Remove dust with a vacuum cleaner

once a year. Rough-textured walls in city homes will need vacuuming twice a year. Sponge off smudges around light switches, etc., with mild detergent solution once a month. Soiled areas above warm-air registers and radiators should be cleaned every couple of months.

If walls are being soiled or scarred by chair backs, doors banging against them, children's bicycles, etc., take steps promptly to fix whatever is causing the damage, or protect the walls with chair rails, doorstops, etc.

To clean greasy walls in the kitchen. The amount of frying you do largely determines how often your kitchen walls and ceilings need to be washed. In some kitchens, semiannual washing is required. In most, however, only annual washing is called for—and even that may not seem necessary; but the point is that if you put off the job until the walls have an obvious grease film, the work becomes very disagreeable and time-consuming, and the results may not be at all satisfactory.

Use a fairly strong detergent solution, and apply to a small area with a sponge (or brush if the wall is textured). Then rinse well. Work from the floor up, and do the ceiling last. If you start at the top of the walls and work down, the detergent may permanently streak the finish lower down.

INTERIOR WALLS, PLASTER

Routine maintenance. As large, unsightly cracks and holes appear, scrape them open, fill with spackle, sand when dry and touch up with paint. (But don't worry about hairline cracks and small holes unless they definitely mar the appearance of the walls. They can wait for repairs until the walls are refinished.)

If paint flakes off in spots and plaster underneath dusts off, search immediately for leaks in the roof, outside walls or plumbing. When these are located and stopped, allow the plaster to dry well before scraping off the crumbs and applying spackle and paint.

174

INTERIOR WALLS—WALLPAPERED AND VINYL-COVERED

Routine maintenance. Remove dust with a vacuum cleaner once a year. If wallpaper is washable, remove smudges with a sponge barely dampened in water or very mild detergent. If wallpaper is not washable, remove soil with a doughlike wallpaper cleaner.

To remove grease. On non-washable paper, make a stiff paste of dry starch and carbon tetrachloride and spread a thick layer on the stain. Allow to dry; then brush off. Repeat treatment as necessary. On partially washable paper, try sponging with a mild detergent. If this doesn't work, apply the same type of poultice. On fully washable paper or vinyl, wash with detergent solution, working from the bottom of the stained area or the bottom of the wall up toward the ceiling. Do not get paper or vinyl too wet, lest you weaken the adhesive at the joints.

If wallpaper comes loose. Lift the edge carefully and spread a little wallpaper paste underneath with a table knife. If you are unable to get a knife underneath, slit the paper at right angles to the loose edge with a razor blade, and then fold the paper back slightly. If the paper is so stiff that it threatens to tear if you lift it, dampen it with water to make it pliable.

It is better not to fix bulges in wallpaper unless they are very unsightly. In that case, dampen with water, slit with a razor blade and spread paste underneath.

INTERIOR WALLS—WATER-TIGHT

Routine maintenance. If cracks develop around the rim of the tub, in the shower recess or at the back of a built-in vanity, scrape them out promptly and fill with silicone calking compound.

See also tile, ceramic and plastic, rigid.

INTERIOR WOODWORK

Maintain like doors (which see).

IRON AND STEEL

Routine maintenance. Dry thoroughly when wet. Then, if

the object is a tool, wipe or spray it lightly with oil. Inspect painted objects regularly and touch up paint if it is thin or cracked.

To remove rust. On painted objects, use a cold chisel, file, knife, sandpaper, emery cloth or steel wool as necessary, or apply a liquid or jellied rust remover. Unpainted objects can be cleaned the same way, though a faster, less laborious method is to drop them into an ultrasonic cleaner. When the last speck of rust is gone, painted objects should be primed with a rust-inhibiting paint and then finished with enamel.

IRONS

Routine maintenance. Remove starch from soleplate when it interferes with smooth ironing by rubbing with fine steel wool. Smooth scratches on the soleplate with very fine emery cloth, and rewax by ironing over several thicknesses of wax paper placed on a newspaper.

KITCHEN COUNTERS

See plastics, rigid; tile, ceramic; stainless steel. To maintain wood cutting blocks, follow directions for taking care of dishwashers (which see) with wood tops.

LAMPS

Routine maintenance. Sponge the lamp bases with water once a year to remove dust and soil. If lamps are handled a great deal, sponge them twice a year with a mild detergent solution to remove skin oils. Remove diffuser bowl and dust or wash every six months. Vacuum shades every two to four weeks. Sponge washable shades about once a year. Reglue lamp-shade trim if it is loosened by the heat of the bulb. Make sure at all times that shades are centered on the lamp; otherwise they will be scorched by the bulbs.

Also see electric cords.

LEATHER

Routine maintenance. If leather is not fastened to a rigid surface, keep it pliable and clean by rubbing with a spray-on

176

Scrape open tiny map cracks in plaster when you repaint rooms and fill them with spackle. A beer-can opener makes an excellent scraper.

leather conditioner or saddle soap every six months. After using soap, rinse well and polish with a dry cloth. Apply furniture wax to tabletops every three to six months, and buff them monthly.

To remove stains. Apply saddle soap or leather conditioner. Grease stains can be removed—sometimes—by covering with rubber cement, which is peeled off when dry. Repeat the treatment as necessary.

LIGHTING FIXTURES

Routine maintenance. If the light is completely enclosed, remove diffusing glass or plastic every six months in order to get out dust and insects. Wash every other cleaning period. If the diffuser is open at the top so that dust and insects can collect in it readily, clean every three months.

Dust all surfaces on which dust settles every month or two. Polished-brass and silver fixtures and black fixtures need most frequent attention. Wash clear-glass shields, such as chimneys on wall fixtures, every other month: even though

177

the glass surfaces are vertical, the dust they collect is high-lighted by the bulb. Dust crystal chandeliers monthly by blowing on them. Wash them every six months to a year.

MARBLE

To remove stains. Grease and oil. Wet stain with Vermarco 50-50 cleaner for a few minutes; then wipe with a dry cloth. If repeated applications do not remove the stain, mix the cleaner with talc to make a thick paste; apply a layer on the stain, and cover with wax paper. After twenty-four hours, remove the poultice and rinse.

Coffee, tea, fruit, wine, tobacco, leaves. Pour Vermarco Hydrogen Peroxide 35 per cent on stain. Add several drops of household ammonia. When bubbling stops, sop up and rinse. Make repeated applications as necessary.

Rust. Apply Vermarco Crystal Cleaner with a sponge. When the stain disappears, rinse with the "A" part of the cleaner.

Paint. Scrape off as much as possible, then apply paint remover. If a stain lingers, bleach with Vermarco Hydrogen Peroxide 35 per cent mixed to a paste with talc and applied as a poultice.

Smoke. Clean with Vermarco Marble Cleaner.

MATTRESSES

Routine maintenance. Turn every three months one side to the other; turn every six months end to end. Vacuum the box spring thoroughly every half year. When buttons come off, retie as soon as possible with coarse linen thread.

To remove urine. Sponge with warm salt water.

To remove odors. This can be very difficult. Try exposing both sides of the mattress to the hot sun on a breezy day.

MIRRORS

Routine maintenance. Dust behind mirrors, if they can be taken down, every other month. Dust frames and glass monthly. When glass is spotted, wash with a damp rag or sponge and polish with a soft, dry rag. If there is an oil film on the glass, wash with a mild detergent solution or a little vinegar in water.

MIXERS

Routine maintenance. Clean thoroughly after every use with a paper towel and damp sponge. Be sure to get off food particles that are embedded in the housing joints, etc.

Remove turntable and clean under it at the same time. Put a drop of salad oil on the turntable spindle every six months. Lubricate motor according to maker's directions—and only if the directions call for it. Straighten beater blades with smooth-jawed pliers whenever they become bent.

OUTDOOR CARPETS

Routine maintenance. Vacuum every couple of days when the carpet is dry. In wet spells, hose it down with strong streams of water; and use a broom to help dislodge accumulated dirt and grit.

To clean. See carpets.

OUTDOOR FURNITURE, CANVAS

Routine maintenance. If the canvas is exposed to the weather, keeping it in presentable condition is almost impossible. This is especially true of light-colored canvas. About the only thing you can do is to wash the canvas frequently—preferably in a machine—with heavy-duty detergent. Use bleach on white canvas.

OUTDOOR FURNITURE, METAL

Routine maintenance. In the spring, scrape off corrosion; sand the bare metal clean; apply an appropriate primer, and repaint. If furniture is exposed to the weather during the summer, complete repainting with an exterior-trim enamel is necessary about every two years.

Dry furniture—especially at the joints—when it is wet. On glass-topped tables, be sure to shove the glass slightly to one side so you can get at the metal rim on which it rests.

If chrome furniture is scratched, apply a chrome cleaner and chrome protector.

OUTDOOR FURNITURE, VINYL

Routine maintenance. Clean as necessary with a detergent solution or vinyl cleaner. Webbed vinyl needs to be washed about every six to eight weeks, because dust and dirt build up rapidly where the strips cross.

OUTDOOR FURNITURE, WOOD, BAMBOO, RATTAN, WICKER

Routine maintenance. Vacuum and clean monthly with a damp rag or mild detergent solution. Dry the furniture well when it is wet by rain or heavy dew. (It is best not to leave the furniture in the open at all, because the sun and rain soon combine to crack the finish and the wood underneath; and the moisture then entering the wood stains it black.)

In the spring, reglue loose joints. Apply a new coat of paint or clear finish (preferably urethane varnish). If wood with a clear finish has become water-stained, apply a commercial bleach to the stained area and sand well when the bleaching process is completed. (But it is much easier to paint over the stain.)

PAVING—DRIVEWAYS, ASPHALT

Asphalt, or blacktop, driveway maintenance, like driveway building, has become a first-class racket. Don't be gulled into paying for maintenance you don't need.

Routine maintenance. If your driveway was properly built according to state highway specifications, little maintenance should be required. Just inspect the paving every spring and every fall for holes and breaks. Fill with packaged blacktop. Fill cracks in the paving with viscous asphalt and scatter a little sand on top before it dries. Scrape off heavy grease, and remove whatever remains with a strong detergent such as Oakite.

If the driveway was an inferior installation, it should be sealed every three or four years by brushing on Jennite. Watch out for cheap (though not always cheap in terms of dollars) imitations of this product. Other maintenance measures are the same as above.

PAVING—DRIVEWAYS, BRICK AND STONE-BLOCK

See brick.

PAVING—DRIVEWAYS, CONCRETE

See concrete.

PAVING—DRIVEWAYS, GRAVEL

Routine maintenance. Rake gravel off adjacent lawn and garden areas at least every fortnight during the mowing season. Level driveway with a rake every second or third month from December through August. When leaves are falling, rake every week. To keep weeds under control, spray the entire driveway with ammonium sulfamate (Ammate) in midspring and again in midsummer. It is usually necessary to add a little new gravel to the driveway about every five years.

PAVING—TERRACES AND WALKS

Routine maintenance. Sweep once or twice a week or clean with an outdoor vacuum. Scrub and hose down the paving once a month. Check and, if necessary, repoint mortar joints every spring with one part cement and two parts sand or with prepared vinyl-concrete patching material.

To kill moss on brick, concrete, porous tile, wood blocks. These materials become extremely slippery when the moss is wet. To kill it, spray with Ammate. The alternative, if there is danger that the Ammate will also kill valuable plants next to the terrace, is to scrub the mossy patches with vinegar or chlorine bleach.

To remove stains. See brick; concrete; carpets; tile, clay.

PEWTER

Routine maintenance. Remove tarnish as necessary with silver polish. If the object is strictly decorative, wax it after cleaning with a white, liquid cleaning wax. This will help to prevent tarnishing for a long period. You may also apply lacquer.

PIANOS

Routine maintenance. Vacuum dust and cobwebs out of the soundbox every month or two. Clean keys as necessary with mild detergent solution. If keys stick, raise the heat and lower the humidity in the room for several days; and work the keys up and down. But don't count on success. Have the piano tuned at least once a year. To maintain the wood surfaces, see furniture, wood.

PICTURES

Routine maintenance. Dust frames and glass monthly. Take down pictures and dust the backs and the wall behind them every other month. Damp-wash glass once a year with a chamois that has been well wrung out in warm water. Take off and polish silver frames every month or two, as they begin to tarnish. Carefully sponge off oil paintings with a sponge or soft cloth wrung out in lukewarm water once a year; but have the paintings thoroughly cleaned by an expert about every ten years.

Inspect oil paintings on canvas annually to make sure canvas is taut. If not, tap in the corner wedges in the back of the frame. Don't try to stretch the canvas very tight.

PLASTICS, RIGID

Routine maintenance. Wash with detergent solution to remove fingermarks, stains, general soil. Don't attempt to remove scratches or burns.

PLUMBING FIXTURES

Routine maintenance. Clean toilet bowl twice a week. Wash other fixtures weekly with detergent solution or non-abrasive cleanser. Touch up chipped spots promptly with porcelain glaze. Remove stains as they occur with household ammonia or with a non-abrasive cleanser such as Zud (which is especially effective for copper and rust stains).

Check for leaks in base of shower stall. If any occur around the rim of the receptor, fill the cracks with silicone calking compound. If leaks are in the bottom, call a plumber fast.

Remove faucet aerators and wash out particles of sediment that collect on the small, round strainers. Replace the parts in the same order that you found them. This little job may be done every three months if your water is full of sediment; only once a year if it is not.

To clean drains. Every family is a law unto itself when it comes to clogging drains. Some through luck or neatness never have any trouble; some clog the kitchen-sink drain but not the lavatory drains; and so on. In other words, you must decide for yourself what your problem is, if any; then you should take routine steps to prevent it.

To keep a sink from clogging—provided you do not have a garbage disposer—pour a little chemical drain cleaner into it every couple of months. If you have a disposer, the ground-up food particles flowing out of it should keep the drain clean (furthermore, a caustic drain cleaner would damage the disposer mechanism).

If your bête noire is the lavatory, lift out the stopper and fish down inside the drain with a stiff wire (such as from a coat hanger) with a small hook on the end. To stop clogging in modern bathtubs, unscrew the escutcheon containing the drain control; lift the entire assembly out of the end of the tub, and clean the wire coil at the bottom of the assembly. In old tubs and shower stalls, about all you can do is to fish down the drain with a hooked wire; or fill the tub or stall with a little water, place the rubber cup of a plumber's friend over the drain opening and pump the handle up and down.

To make a toilet operate properly. If water runs steadily into the bowl after flushing, remove tank top and adjust the rod on the stopper ball and the guides for the rod so that the ball falls squarely into the seat. If the ball is old and flabby, replace it.

If the tank does not fill enough so that the bowl is not flushed clean, bend slightly upward the rod to which the large float is attached.

If the tank fills so much that water flows into the overflow pipe, bend the float rod slightly downward. If the overflow continues, unscrew the float and if it is full of water, replace it with a new one.

To unclog a shower head. Modern shower heads rarely clog; but old ones often do when the water is hard or full of sediment. If the flow from a shower head starts to dwindle, try to remove the face of the head, or the entire head, and scrape the encrusted salts from the back of the face. If removal of the head is impossible, clean the ports by sticking a pin through them every four to six months.

To stop faucet drips. If you have modern faucets, dripping is unusual. It is also pretty tricky to stop. Better call a plumber. But if you have old-fashioned compression faucets, the job is easy: Shut off the valve controlling the flow to the faucet. Remove the faucet handle and unscrew the big packing nut below it. Screw out the stem assembly and replace the washer at the bottom end; then reassemble.

PLUMBING FIXTURES—SHOWER CURTAINS AND SHOWER DOORS

Routine maintenance. Take down curtains and scrub them with detergent solution every other month to remove soap and to prevent mildewing.

Clean tracks in which tub doors slide with a toothbrush and detergent solution every half year. Wash clear-glass doors with warm water about once a week, or polish them well with a dry towel. Translucent doors need to be cleaned only about every two months.

PLUMBING SYSTEM

Routine maintenance. In areas where the temperature drops below freezing in winter, shut off the water to all outside faucets in the fall. If the shut-off valve has a drain plug (as it should), open the plug and drain off the water left in the pipe. If the valve lacks a drain plug leave the faucet open.

To control water hammer. If pipes thump when a faucet is partly turned on or abruptly turned off, make sure the large packing nut on the faucet nearest the thumping sound is tight and that the faucet washer is sound. If thumping continues, shut off the main supply valve, open all faucets and drain the entire system. This will allow air to enter the pipes and act as a cushion against the thumping.

To stop leaks around handles of shut-off valves. Tighten

New kitchen range surface is made of flat smooth, easy-to-clean glass ceramic. The heating elements are sealed beneath the glass. (Corning Glass Works)

the cap nuts with a wrench. If this doesn't work, remove the nuts and wrap graphite wicking or cotton string around the valve stem; then replace the nuts.

To drain the plumbing system. This is necessary if you shut up the house in the winter; otherwise the pipes may freeze, burst and flood the place. Part of the job is simple; part is anything but. Hire a plumber.

RANGES

Routine maintenance. Wipe up spills and grease splatters on the range surface when they occur. Drip pans under burners should also be cleaned right after boil-overs occur; but since you may not be aware of every boil-over, it's a good idea to inspect and wash the pans once a week. Use a strong detergent solution and scouring pads as necessary. Clean gas burners weekly with a damp cloth; and if the ports appear to be clogged, remove the burners and wash in detergent solution.

Clean the drip pan below the cooking top every month. Grease that accumulates on it may become hot enough to ignite and burn wires, controls, etc. Clean oven vent duct at the same time.

Clean oven and broiler with detergent solution whenever there are food spills or grease splatters. Wait until the oven is cool, of course. Rinse well, because detergent or soap may leave new stains on oven walls. If food becomes cooked on the oven walls in spots, wipe with ammonia to soften it; or put a bowl of ammonia in oven overnight. Then wash with detergent and rinse.

If oven is very dirty, clean with whatever oven cleaner you favor and rinse well.

If you have a self-cleaning oven, operate it in accordance with the manufacturer's directions. Drip pans under surface units can also be cleaned in the oven.

RECORD PLAYERS

Routine maintenance. Dust and polish like furniture, wood. Replace stylus of cartridge before it has worn down enough to damage your records. A diamond-tipped stylus given average use should be checked under a microscope every year, though it may not need replacement that often. A sapphire-tipped stylus lasts for only about 50 hours of playing.

Remove turntable about once a year and dust under it carefully.

REFRIGERATORS

Routine maintenance. Wash doors with a mild detergent solution every fortnight; and apply a white, liquid cleaning wax—at least around the handles—every two months. Wash other exterior surfaces—especially the door gaskets and the top of the refrigerator—every month. Pull refrigerator out from the wall at least once a year; clean space behind and under it; and wash the usually hidden sides of the refrigerator. Spot-wash the interior of the refrigerator and freezer compartments once a month and thorough-clean both compartments at least once a year. Use a detergent solution; follow with a solution of one teaspoon baking soda in one quart water; and then rinse well. Clean space housing the refrigerator mechanism with a vacuum cleaner twice a year. Wash the evaporator pan at the same time. When washing plastic or glass parts, avoid using very hot water. Never use scouring cleansers on ice trays or pour boiling hot liquids into them.

Defrost manual-defrost refrigerators every one to four weeks depending on how fast the frost builds up on the ice-cube compartment. Defrosting should be done when the frost is about ¼-inch thick. Do not use a sharp instrument to dislodge the ice or an electric heater to melt it.

ROOF DECKS

Routine maintenance. Sweep once or twice a week when the deck is in use. Sweep off leaves and twigs in the fall and winter. Depending on the amount of wear, apply deck paint every year or two to canvas. If a rubber deck becomes scratched or thin in spots, brush on a new coat of rubber.

Examine the legs of roof-deck furniture once or twice during the summer to make sure they cannot puncture or damage the deck surface.

ROOFS—ALL TYPES

Routine maintenance. If you take a good, hard look at your entire roof every fall, you may be able to forestall a lot of expensive trouble. Known problems that arise between these inspections should, of course, be corrected immediately.

If it is possible to get up on the roof without breaking your neck, sweep off leaves and twigs which may serve as dams in winter and bring on leaks.

To kill moss on roofs. Moss will grow on any kind of roof, especially if it is in a damp, shaded location; but it is most commonly seen on wood shingles. To kill it, scrape it off, taking pains not to damage the roofing. Then spray or brush a preservative containing pentachlorophenol (Woodlife or Pentaseal, for example) on a wood roof. Treat other roofs with 2 pounds sodium pentachlorophenate dissolved in 5 gallons water or with ½ ounce sodium arsenite in 10 gallons water. Be very careful not to get any of these solutions on plants. Retreat the roof when moss starts to grow again.

ROOFS, ASBESTOS-CEMENT

See exterior walls, asbestos-cement.

ROOFS, ASPHALT SHINGLE

To stop a leak. Lift shingle carefully and spread asphalt roofing cement on the hole underneath. If the hole is large, insert a piece of aluminum flashing over it. The flashing should extend up beyond the butt of the shingle in the next course above.

If butts are curled. Glue them down with asphalt roofing cement; otherwise the wind may get under them and rip the shingles.

To add life to a sound but old and somewhat worn roof. Brush on an asphalt-base aluminum roofing paint. Use a thick paint containing fibers if the old roofing has small cracks and holes. Use a thin, non-fibered paint on other roofs. Beware of so-called miracle plastic, rubber or elastomeric coatings that are said to renew all types of roof for an incredible period of time.

188

ROOFS, BUILT-UP TAR AND GRAVEL

To stop leaks. Scrape the gravel to one side; apply asphalt roofing cement to the hole, and spread the gravel on it.

ROOFS, FIBERGLASS

To stop leaks at seams between panels. Loosen the top panel; clean out old calking compound, and apply a clear sealer available from fiberglass-roofing dealers.

ROOFS, METAL

Routine maintenance. Repaint a galvanized steel roof every three to four years; a terne roof every ten years. If a natural-finish aluminum roof begins to corrode badly, it should be painted like a steel roof. Metal roofs with a factory-applied, baked-on finish need little attention; but if the finish is damaged, you should apply a primer and finish paint promptly.

To stop leaks. If holes are small, clean the surface around them and apply plastic steel. Large holes should be attended to by a sheet-metal worker.

ROOFS, RUBBER

To stop leaks. Brush on a new coat of rubber.

ROOFS, SLATE AND TILE

To stop leaks. Slip a piece of aluminum flashing under the slate or tile, over the hole. Hold in place with asphalt roofing cement. If a slate or tile is broken, however, call in a roofing contractor.

ROOFS, WOOD SHINGLE

To stop a leak. Insert a piece of aluminum flashing under the shingle, over the hole. The metal should extend up beyond the butts of the shingles in the next course above.

Shingles with a stained finish. It is not necessary to stain wood shingles, although some people do it to achieve a certain color and/or to lengthen their life slightly. If your shingles are stained and you wish to keep them that way,

189

they should be restained every five years with a stain mixed with a wood preservative. You can, however, stop the stain treatment at any time.

SCREENS

Routine maintenance. Dust and wash screens every spring. Scrub copper, galvanized steel and unfinished-aluminum screen cloth with a brush; then apply one or two coats of spar varnish or screen paint to the first two. In coastal areas, it is advisable to varnish aluminum screen cloth, too. Apply the finish with a scrap of carpet to avoid clogging the mesh.

Scrape and apply exterior-trim paint to wood frames as necessary. During the summer, wash wood doorframes every month—especially around the knob and on upper edges of the rails, where dirt collects.

If screen cloth begins to belly badly along one edge, pry off the molding covering the edge and tighten and restaple the cloth. If you fail to do this promptly, further pressure on the cloth is likely to make it unravel to a point where it must be replaced entirely.

To repair small holes in screen cloth. If no wires—or only a few—are broken, simply push them together with a pencil point. For a larger hole, buy a metal-screen patch and hook it into place.

To store. Careful storage protects screens against accidental damage and keeps wood screens from warping. The best procedure—and usually the most practical—is to lay the screens flat, one atop another, in wide, U-shaped wood racks suspended from the basement or garage ceiling joists. If screen hardware, such as hooks and knobs, prevents one screen frame from touching the next at all points, separate them with boards—two for window screens; three for door screens.

SEPTIC SYSTEMS

Routine maintenance. The frequency with which septic tanks must be cleaned varies with the size of the tank, the size of the family and the habits of the household. Until

190

you have learned from experience exactly how often your septic tank needs to be pumped out, it is advisable to open it once a year. If the total depth of the scum and solids exceeds one-third of the liquid depth of the tank, the solids should be removed. Most homeowners need to clean their tanks every other year; but you might be able to go longer.

Cleaning must be done by a septic-tank cleaning service. Chemicals are of no value. To speed the cleaning service's work and perhaps avoid extra charges, keep a diagram showing the location of your tank and distribution field; and drive a stake into the ground directly above the opening to the tank.

SHELVES

Routine maintenance. Dust open shelves every two to four weeks; shelves behind doors every four to six months.

Painted shelves and, to a lesser extent, stained shelves are rather quickly soiled by books and records which are pushed and pulled across them. To minimize this problem, apply a white, liquid cleaning wax once a month. Only the front edges and exposed top areas require waxing.

SHUTTERS

Routine maintenance. Inspect catches once a year to make sure they are sound: if a shutter breaks loose in a storm, it may batter itself and the adjacent window frame badly. Scrubbing and hosing down shutters at least once a year will remove unsightly dirt and help to preserve the paint; even so, repainting is generally required every two or three years.

SILLS

Routine maintenance. Inspect annually for termites and rot. To make sure there is no trouble, poke an ice pick into the wood at frequent intervals. If wood is rotten at the surface in scattered spots, cut it out with a chisel and slather the sound wood with wood preservative. Apply preservative to all other exposed surfaces also.

191

SILVER

Routine maintenance. Remove tarnish as necessary with silver polish—preferably a paste or liquid that you apply with a soft cloth rather than an electrolytic cleaner, which slowly destroys the silver. In using a paste or liquid, rub the silver up and down rather than across or round and round. An ultrasonic cleaner may also be used to remove tarnish without any effort on your part; but never use it for worn silverplate.

If silver is not on display or in regular use, keep it wrapped in a silver bag, tarnish-resistant paper or cloth. This will slow the development of tarnish.

STAINLESS STEEL

Routine maintenance. Clean as necessary with a detergent solution. Scratches can sometimes be obliterated with very fine emery cloth, but it's a risky business and you might make the surface worse than it was.

STAIRS

Routine maintenance. See floors, wood for care of wood and stone treads. See carpets for care of carpeted treads. If wood risers are exposed, remove rubber-heel marks and other smudges with a white, liquid cleaning wax or with a strong detergent such as Fantastik. This may have to be done as often as every fortnight on stairs with very shallow treads but only every six months on stairs with very deep treads. Similarly, you may have to refinish the risers every year, or only every five or six years.

Wipe the stair railing with a cloth dampened in mild detergent solution every month. Dust turned balusters and around the base of all balusters at the same time.

Sanding and refinishing of clear-finished or painted treads may be required every year or two. Carpet may require replacement every four or five years.

STONE

Routine maintenance. See exterior walls, masonry.
To remove stains. See brick.

Ultrasonic cleaners clean by transmitting ultrasonic energy through a fluid. This forms millions of tiny bubbles which scrub articles in the cleaning tank in short order. The cleaner removes dirt, grease, tarnish, stains and rust from almost any hard or semi-hard article, but does not clean fabrics. (Branson Instruments)

STORM SASH

Routine maintenance. In the fall, before hanging the sash, inspect and repair glazing compound; wash glass and frames. Repaint wood frames every three or four years. Remove rust from extension arms on tilt-out windows and apply a drop of oil. Adjust pneumatic closers on doors so that they close firmly but not with a shattering crash. Check and repair calking around frames of combination windows every year, and clean the aluminum tracks at the same time. If the windows are old and the tracks somewhat corroded, making the glass insets hard to move, sand the tracks and rub them with paraffin or spray with a silicone lubricant.

To store. See screens.

SUMP PUMPS

Routine mainenance. Remove pump once a year to clean the intake and remove any matter that has accumulated in the sump. Fill the sump with water to make sure the pump is operating properly.

TELEVISION ANTENNA

Routine maintenance. Unless you like to wander around on rooftops, leave repairs to an expert. But at least take a look at the antenna a couple of times a year (use binoculars if necessary) to make sure it is properly secured, reasonably upright, aimed in the right direction, has not been damaged by falling tree limbs or wind, and is attached firmly to the lead-in wire.

TELEVISION RECEIVER

Routine maintenance. Dust when you dust the rest of the furniture. Wash smudges off plastic and metal cabinets with a mild detergent solution every couple of months; and apply a white, liquid cleaning wax every four months. Treat a wood cabinet like the furniture piece it is (see furniture, wood). Sponge off the screen with detergent solution every month if you have small children; about every six months otherwise. Clean controls at the same times.

TILE, CERAMIC

Routine maintenance. How often you should wash tile depends, obviously, on how fast it shows dirt or simply looks dull, blotched and streaked. Kitchen counters usually need to be washed once or twice a day; bathroom floors and shower-stall walls, once a week; the wall behind a lavatory, once a fortnight; other bathroom walls, once every couple of months. As a rule, a sponge or cloth dipped in water removes all soil on the tiles themselves (except in kitchen counters, where you need a detergent). But to clean the grout, you should at every third or fourth washing use a fairly strong detergent solution. If the grout becomes quickly and badly stained by grease and impurities in your water—a common problem—monthly cleaning with a brush and ceramic-tile liquid cleaner, such as Afta, is necessary. In all cases, after the tiles are washed, dry them vigorously to make them sparkle.

If mortar joints become cracked or crumbly, scrape them open and fill with white tile cement.

To remove other stains. Rust. Scrub with any liquid or jellied rust remover, and rinse well.

Rubber heel marks. Scrub with an abrasive cleanser.

Nail polish. Use a nail-polish remover.

Paint. Scrape with a razor blade. In hard-to-get-at spots, use a paint remover.

Grease. This normally comes up with a detergent. If not, scrub with a strong solution of washing soda; let the solution stand on the tile for an hour; then rinse.

Coffee, blood, mustard, ink. Scrub with a copious amount of household bleach; then rinse.

TILE, QUARRY

See floors, quarry tile. To remove stains, see tile, ceramic.

TOASTERS

Routine maintenance. Clean out crumb tray every month or so. At the same time, turn the toaster upside down and allow any crumbs left inside to fall out (but don't shake the poor toaster to pieces).

195

To clean. See chrome-plated steel.

VACUUM CLEANERS

Routine maintenance. Inspect revolving brush occasionally and remove threads and strings which have wrapped around it. Turn cloth dirt bag inside out once a month and shake off dirt. Don't wash it.

If suction is poor when the dirt bag is empty, dirt is undoubtedly clogging the machine at some other point. If you have a canister cleaner, attach the hose to the blower end of the canister and try to blow out the obstruction. If this does not work, clean the hose with a long, stiff wire. Be careful not to poke the wire through the sides of the hose. If you have an upright cleaner, take off the dirt bag, and clean the outlet in the head of the machine with a wire.

VENETIAN BLINDS

Routine maintenance. Dust or vacuum blinds every time you dust your furniture. To do the job, drop the blinds all the way down and adjust the slats downward until they are almost closed; clean; then reverse the slats and clean again.

When slats become greasy, sponge them with a cloth wrung out in detergent solution. Adjust the slats downward and upward as when dusting. Finish cleaning by opening the slats wide and washing around and behind the tapes. Be careful not to dirty the tapes.

When the tapes finally become too grimy to bear, take down the blinds and replace the tapes or, better, send the blinds to a Venetian blind cleaning service.

VINYL WALLCOVERINGS

See interior walls, wallpapered and vinyl-covered.

WAFFLE IRONS

Routine maintenance. Never wash or scour the grids; just wipe with a paper towel. To clean the exterior, see chrome-plated steel.

WALLPAPER

See interior walls, wallpapered and vinyl-covered.

WASHERS

Routine maintenance. After every use, wipe off the top, the lid and the hinges of the lid with a damp cloth; then dry—the hinges especially, since they sometimes rust. Clean control panel about once a month. Clean front and sides of washer with a mild detergent solution every couple of months.

Remove the agitator once a month and clean the inside of it well. Also clean the agitator post. Then apply a little vaseline to the screw threads to which the agitator cap is screwed.

On a wringer washer, wipe the wringer rolls with a damp cloth after each use, and release the tension on them.

WATER HEATERS

Routine maintenance. Drain a pailful of water from a tank-type water heater every two or three months. Have the burner on an oil-fired heater serviced annually. Make sure the flue pipe from a gas or oil heater to the chimney is not corroded or separated at the joints.

Tankless heaters do not require very much maintenance until the flow of hot water regularly slackens when the faucets are turned on. (This may never happen if your water is soft, however.) Then you must call in a serviceman to purge the heater coils with acid.

WATER SYSTEMS

Routine maintenance if you have your own well and pump. Lubricate pump according to the manufacturer's directions. Adjust the air cushion in the pressure tank if the pump goes on and off frequently when a faucet is open (a sure indication that the tank is waterlogged—does not have an adequate air cushion), or if the water comes out in violent bursts (an indication that the air cushion is too large). The adjustment is made in different ways, depending on the design of the pump and water system and also on whether the system is equipped with an automatic air control. Follow the manufacturer's or pump dealer's directions.

Routine maintenance. Dry horizontal wood and steel mullions as soon as inner-glass surface on which condensation has formed cease to drip. This will help to prevent rusting of steel frames and rapid destruction of paint or stain on both wood and steel.

Refinish wood and steel windows outside and in about every five or six years. Clean aluminum frames as necessary with an aluminum cleaner. If aluminum is covered with a transparent finish, apply new finish on the exterior surfaces of the frame every two or three years; on interior surfaces, every six to eight years.

Lubricate hinges and adjust arms on casement, awning and jalousie windows once a year. If wood double-hung windows tend to stick in summer, rub paraffin on the stiles or spray with a silicone lubricant several times in the spring and summer. Every three or four months, clean tracks in which horizontal windows slide and apply paraffin to them every year.

Replace all windowpanes when cracked or broken.

To wash windows. If your windows have small panes, measure their width and buy a rubber squeegee for each different size. For large panes and picture windows, buy a twelve-inch squeegee—anything wider is extremely difficult to handle.

When washing, add a couple of tablespoonfuls vinegar or ammonia to one gallon water, or mix one tablespoonful non-abrasive household cleaner in one gallon water. Wet a sponge in the solution and wring it out well; then rub it on the glass. How many panes you can wash at once depends on how dry the weather is.

Before a pane starts to dry, hold the rubber edge of a squeegee of the proper size against the glass at the top of the pane, and pull it quickly and firmly downward till you reach the bottom mullion. Then, with a damp chamois, wipe off the squeegee and the bottom mullion. Proceed to the next pane.

On windows with large panes, make several downward

strokes with the squeegee. The strokes should overlap about an inch. Wipe the squeegee between each stroke and wipe off the bottom mullion when the window is clean.

After washing only a few windows, you will find that this window-washing method is much the fastest and easiest you have ever used. It also gives the best results.

In the case of jalousies, however, the squeegee is of no value. In fact, there isn't any perfect way to wash jalousies. The best you can do is to open the windows wide; run over the top and bottom of each louver with a wet sponge; and dry with a chamois.

WINDOW SHADES

Routine maintenance. Clean shades as necessary. If they are of washable material, take them down and lay them on a large, flat surface. Wash with a sponge wrung out in mild detergent solution. If fabric is not washable, erase the dirt with a dough-type wallpaper cleaner.

If a shade does not roll all the way to the top of the window, pull it two-thirds down; remove the roller from the brackets; roll the shade up by hand, and reset it in the brackets. Repeat the process if the shade still balks.

If the shade snaps up violently when released, raise it to the top; remove from the brackets, unroll by hand to half the shade's length; and replace in the brackets. Repeat as necessary.

6

Home-Maintenance Services You May Want to Use

Economists and business writers make much of the fact that this is the age of service. Everywhere you turn, new businesses that sell services rather than products are popping up. Since about 1950, service businesses as a group have made proportionally faster growth than manufacturing businesses, farming, etc.

Home-maintenance services have played a part in this interesting development. But I question whether it has been a terribly big part, for although the total number of home-maintenance firms has burgeoned, the types of service they offer today are not very different from those that have been available for a good many years. Furthermore, maintenance services have had downs and ups as homeowners gained and lost and regained interest in doing-it-yourself.

Be that as it may, home-maintenance services in large numbers are available almost everywhere. Here is a list. It may give you some ideas for solving or preventing certain maintenance problems.

Home-Repair Services
  Bricklayers
  Carpenters
  Countertop makers
  Driveway contractors
  Dry-wall contractors and tapers (the former can make all dry-wall repairs: the latter are concerned only with the tape and plaster used to conceal joints and nailheads)
  Electrical contractors (also repair electric heating installations)
  Excavating contractors (needed in case you must replace a water main, for example)
  Fence dealers
  Floor layers (for repairing wood floors; usually also refinish floors)
  Floor-sanding and -refinishing services (for wood floors)
  Garage-door dealers
  Glass dealers (for replacing windowpanes and refinishing mirrors)
  Insulation contractors
  Locksmiths
  Marble contractors
  Masons (generally can handle any work involving concrete)
  Painters
  Paperhangers
  Plasterers
  Plumbers (also repair hot-water and steam heating systems)
  Resilient-flooring contractors (usually listed in the Yellow Pages under linoleum dealers)
  Roofers or roofing contractors (also repair gutters and leaders)
  Seamless-flooring contractors
  Sheet-metal contractors (work on flashing, ducts, metal roofs; might also work on metal siding)
  Shower-door dealers
  Siding contractors
  Spray-painting services (for repainting kitchen cabinets and appliances)
  Storm sash dealers
  Terrazzo contractors
  Tilesetters or ceramic-tile contractors
  Ventilating contractors
  Waterproofing contractors
  Window-screen dealers

Equipment Repair and Maintenance Services
  Air-conditioning contractors
  Heating contractors, gas utilities, LP-gas dealers, fuel-oil deal-

ers, electrical contractors, plumbers. (If you burn gas, LP-gas or oil, it is usually best to seek service first from the fuel dealer; then, if he cannot help you, call in a heating contractor for a warm-air system or a plumber for a hot-water or steam system. If you heat with electricity, your first contact is an electrical contractor; but heating contractors and even insulating contractors are also getting into the elecric-heat business.)

Major-appliance services (usually listed in the Yellow Pages under the names of specific appliances: refrigerators, washers, etc.)

Motor-repair services (if you need to repair large motors for water pumps, swimming pools, etc.)

Radio and television services

Small-appliance services

Water-pump dealers

Water softening-equipment dealers or water treating services

Other Repair and Maintenance Services

Antique-repair and -refinishing services

Art-restoring services (also work on picture frames)

Awning-repair services

Bookbinders

Chair-caning services (also usually repair rush seats)

Clock-repair services

Dyers

Furniture-repair and -refinishing services

Invisible weavers

Lamp-repair services

Lamp shade-repair services

Marble dealers (for repairing and refinishing marble-topped tables and other portable pieces; but use a marble contractor for repairing marble floors and other built-ins)

Mattress-rebuilding services

Photo-restoring services

Piano tuners

Pillow-renovating services

Seamstresses

Silversmiths (repair and replate silver and other metals; also clean very dirty or heavily tarnished metals. Jewelers also can help you with your precious-metal problems; but only the largest firms actually do their own work)

Taxidermists (to repair that old moose head)

Upholsterers

Vacation home-maintenance services (more than just caretakers—they see that problems which arise while the house is empty are corrected before you return)

Venetian blind-repair services
Welding services (to repair iron railings, iron furniture, etc.)
Wicker shops (to repair rattan, reed and willow furniture)

Cleaning Services
Building cleaners (use sandblasting and steam-cleaning equipment to clean masonry surfaces)
Chimney cleaners
Crystal-chandelier cleaners
Drapery cleaners
Dry cleaners
Floor-waxing services
Fur cleaners (for fur rugs as well as fur coats)
Furnace-cleaning services (offered by heating contractors and fuel-oil dealers)
Furniture and upholstery cleaners (these firms usually clean carpets and rugs also)
Gutter-cleaning services (make simple adjustments as well as cleaning; but major repairs are best done by a roofing contractor)
House cleaners (work inside the house, on everything)
Laundries
Marble contractors
Metal-cleaning services
Oil tank-cleaning services
Rug and carpet cleaners (some carpet dealers also do cleaning)
Septic tank-cleaning services
Sewer-cleaning services
Terrazzo contractors
Venetian blind dealers

Other Services
Exterminators
Fumigators
Odor neutralizers

Reading down this impressive list, you probably find yourself wondering about the services listed:

What do they cost? My only answer can be: "They're not cheap." Service businesses use a great deal of labor and not much of anything else; and I don't need to tell you that in recent years, labor rates have been going through the roof.

In 1968, in the very expensive town of Greenwich, Connecticut, we paid nine dollars to have our kitchen floor cleaned and waxed. In 1969, in a tiny town in eastern Connecticut, where all costs—except of food—are generally lower, we paid twelve dollars to have a kitchen floor of almost identical size cleaned and waxed.

In other words, service costs vary between communities as well as from year to year. There is also considerable variation between types of services.

How good is the service you get? On the average, only fair. Service businesses today are having a hard time attracting and holding help. As a result, many of the service-firm employees who do work for you lack the skill, experience and desire to do good work. This is particularly true when the work involved calls for relatively little skill.

By and large, it has been my experience that the best service is given by men and women who own and operate their own businesses without any help. True, they may not always be so fast getting to your problem as you'd like; but when they do, they do the job well and quickly—and they stand behind it.

Then what's the advantage of hiring a service? Obviously there are many jobs you cannot do yourself because they are technical, call for considerable strength or agility, require special equipment, etc.

There are also sound reasons for employing a service to do work you can easily do yourself: You can devote your time and energy to other more important things. And in many cases, you don't have to load up with equipment and supplies needed for the job.

Are there any advantages to hiring a real service firm rather than, say, a general handyman or cleaning woman? The firm sees to it that the workers you need get to your home. That means you don't have to pick anyone up or pay his carfare. You don't have to pay for social security—that's the service firm's responsibility. And you are not called upon to provide lunch.

I do not claim, however, that the work you get from the service firm's workers necessarily will be as good as that you expect from faithful old Sam, that superlative jack-of-all-trades who has worked for you for years.

Before engaging a service to work in or around your home,

what should you find out about it? First, you should ask for whom it has previously worked. Then you should check up on what those previous customers think of it. I realize that many people do not do this. I don't always myself. But you are flying blind if you don't.

If the servicemen are going to work inside the house, you ought to determine whether they are bonded. True, they may be perfectly honest if they're not. But a bond is an added protection.

Finally, you should make sure that the owner of the service firm is fully insured against accidents to himself and his men.

Should you arrange for routine cleaning work on a regular basis? If so, how often should you have service? If you're satisfied with the work the cleaning service does, by all means arrange with it to come to you on a more or less set schedule. Then you can be pretty sure it will not willingly let you down.

But if you call for service only at the last minute, on an erratic schedule, it won't make any difference whether you are a regular customer or not: There will be times when you won't get service because the firm simply cannot schedule its operations to accommodate you.

Another advantage of having regular service is that the service people know what they did "last time" and can do something else "this time" if repetition of work is not obviously needed.

How often you should schedule a cleaning service depends on the cost of the service, the size and efficiency of the crew, the size and complexity of your house and the number of people living in the house. You can probably make a good guess about the schedule you need; but you really should work it out with the service manager.

Should you buy a service contract on major items of equipment such as appliances, TV sets and heating systems? Service contracts, or agreements, are a form of insurance. Their purpose is to assure that you will get service on your mechanical equipment after the warranty runs out. Each piece of equipment is, as a rule, covered by a separate contract; and the cost and conditions of the contracts, which run for one year, vary with the firms that issue them. They also vary with the equipment covered, your address and your requirements. For example:

—you may be able to buy a contract that gives you inspection only; or inspection and labor to make any needed repairs; or inspection, labor and parts.

—you may be able to buy a contract only when the equipment is under a certain age; or you may be turned down on equipment which, regardless of age, is deemed to be in bad shape; or you may be required to bring equipment up to standard before a contract is issued.

—you may pay more for a contract if you live, say, at the seashore, where metal is rapidly corroded by salt air, than inland.

—in 1970 you might have paid $8.50 for a labor-and-parts contract on a one-door refrigerator entering its second year; $79.50 for a labor-and-parts contract on a three-ton year-round air conditioner; $30 for a labor-and-parts contract on an oil burner; $60 for a labor-and-parts contract on a new television set; $135 for a labor-and-parts contract on a three-year-old television set. (These are actual charges made by different firms in different parts of the country.)

There is no sound basis for deciding whether you should take out service contracts on your equipment. Temperament and past experience are your only guides. If you're a fatalist, you probably favor service contracts. If you're an optimist, you probably don't. But these points are worth noting:

1. The majority of firms issuing service contracts expect to make money on them. This means that their service records tell them that their customers *as a group* will require less service than they paid for. Of course, some individual customers will require more than they pay for; and maybe you will be one of them. But then again, maybe you won't be.

The only companies issuing service contracts that do not expect a profit from them are fuel-oil dealers. True, they price their contracts as nearly as possible to break even. But their main reason for offering contracts is to keep your oil burner in good shape so you will continue to buy oil from them.

2. Another reason why service contracts on appliances, air conditioners and gas heating equipment are priced high is

that the issuing firms know a certain number of contract holders will demand service they don't need. (For example, if Mrs. Jones has a service contract on a refrigerator, and the refrigerator suddenly stops, she may call for service even though her trouble stems from a blown fuse which she herself could replace in thirty seconds.) In other words, if people called for service only when they really needed it, service contracts would probably come down slightly in price. But unfortunately people are not likely to change their give-me-service-on-everything attitude very soon.

3. The representative for a large California association of television-repair firms told me recently that, in order to justify the cost of service contracts, companies offering them fix only what needs fixing when you call for help, and they don't mind coming back when something else goes wrong the next day. By contrast, he said, independent repair dealers must struggle to survive, so when you call them for help, they not only fix what needs fixing, but they also look for anything else that might soon go wrong and they fix that at the same time. This is a form of preventive maintenance which saves the customer the annoyance of making several calls for service, and in the long run, saves him money for labor costs.

Whether this charge against contract issuers is justified I do not know. Certainly it does not square with the issuers' desire to make money on their contracts. On the other hand, firms offering contracts are usually large, and their servicemen are not always imbued with the idea of saving them money.

4. As opposed to these arguments against service contracts, you should remember that if you hold a contract on a piece of equipment, you are more likely to get prompt service than if you don't.

5. Finally—and unhappily—you must face up to the fact that household equipment today seems to require more service than ever before. This is partly because there is more in use; partly because the equipment is much more complicated; and partly because it isn't well made in the first place.

Consider the fact that a recent statewide survey of California's independent television-repair dealers showed that in the first ninety days after the average TV set is purchased, it requires 1.5 repair calls. In the remaining nine months of the year, it requires 2.3 additional repair calls. In the second year, it requires 3 repair calls. And in the third year the figure goes still higher.

Or consider the fact that complaints coming to the federal government and Better Business bureaus in the past few years indicate that refrigerators—once considered almost as trouble-free as any major appliance made—are now the most unreliable.

Yes, it's a confusing world. And the value of service contracts is one of the more confusing aspects of it.

If you press me for an answer to the original question— "Should you buy a service contract on major items of equipment?"—I can give you only my unsubstantiated personal opinion:

On appliances and television sets, no. On year-round air conditioners, yes—but I'd buy inspection (two a year) and labor only. On oil burners, by all means, because the contracts provide the annual cleaning and overhaul that all oil burners must have to operate properly.

Does it pay to rent equipment, such as water heaters and gas burners, in order to get free service? Not unless your contract provides that ownership of the appliances will be transferred to you when the total of the rent you have paid equals the purchase price of the appliances. If you just keep on paying rent month after month, year after year, you will probably eventually reach a point where you are pouring money down the drain.

The appliances that utilities rent out are not cheap models that require much service; they are, on the contrary, first-class models that require very little service. Therefore, when you rent an appliance from a utility in order to save money on service, you are betting against the odds.

In other words, the main reason for renting an appliance is not to save money on service but to avoid a substantial expenditure for the appliance and its installation.

Index